D1087436

Order and Dispute

Simon Roberts was educated at Tonbridge School and then at the London School of Economics, where he took a degree in law. He became interested in legal anthropology while teaching at a newly established law school in Malawi, and subsequently spent two years doing field research in Botswana. He has written *Tswana Family Law* (1972) and edited *Law and the Family in Africa* (1977). He is married with two children and presently teaches in the Law Department at the London School of Economics.

Simon Roberts

Order and Dispute

An Introduction to Legal Anthropology

St. Martin's Press · New York

Library of Congress Cataloging in Publication Data

Robert, Simon.
      Order and dispute.

      Bibliography: p.
      Includes index.
      1. Law, Primitive. 2. Ethnological jurispru-
dence. 3. Justice, Administration of. I. Title.
K190.R6   304.1'15   78–24778
ISBN 0–312–58713–9

For Marian

Contents

Preface

Even if Malinowski could fairly complain in 1934 that the anthropology of law had been neglected 'to an extent which the layman would find unbelievable and which the specialist realizes with shock',[1] this deficiency has long been made up. His own vivid writings on the subject preceded books by Llewellyn and Hoebel, Schapera, Gluckman, Turner, Bohannan and Gulliver which have all come to be regarded as classics of their kind. Some good textbooks, collections of essays and selected readings have followed, but there is still nothing of an introductory nature beyond some terse chapters in books on general anthropology and a few rather inadequate sections on 'historical jurisprudence' in works of legal theory. So my primary object here is to provide something for the newcomer, whether an interested layman or the prospective student.

Despite the sub-title, it must be said at the start that this is not a book about law. Two quite distinct traditions of scholarship have grown up under the general label of 'legal anthropology'; one explicitly concerned with law, and another with broader questions of order in society. Despite a legal education, my own sympathies are firmly in the latter camp, as I doubt the value of attempting to isolate the 'legal' as a generic field of study in the small-scale societies with which this book is concerned. The approach adopted here has meant abandoning familiar legal perspectives and modes of analysis, and then feeling my way among those developed in other social sciences; as a result, some of the arguments are likely to appear naïve and stilted to the professional.

Quite apart from questions of perspective, this does not pretend to be a comprehensive survey of the field. In particular,

1. Introduction to Hogbin, *Law and Order in Polynesia*, p. lxi.

I have neglected the important subjects of pluralism and change; and said nothing about the relationships of these small-scale societies to those larger nation states within which they are now all encapsulated. Nor is the growing interest of anthropologists in the legal systems of contemporary western societies reflected here at all. Some readers of the manuscript complained vigorously about these omissions; but introductions to these topics can be found elsewhere, and an adequate treatment of them here could only have been provided by leaving out other material which I felt it essential to include.

Anyone attempting an introduction to legal anthropology must owe a huge debt to the scholars I mentioned at the beginning, and also to the major attempts at synthesis by Nader[2] and Abel.[3] There is also a more immediate debt to Isaac Schapera, who gave constant encouragement and expert help; it is a pity he could not have been persuaded to write a book on 'law' himself. At Penguin, Jill Norman provided friendly assistance throughout. This book grew in conjunction with a course of lectures at L.S.E., and numerous students in successive years read and commented on drafts as these were prepared. Later, as something like a final form appeared, several good friends agreed to read it, particularly Stuart Anderson, Simon Coldham, Patrick McAuslan and David Schiff. I am very grateful for the help they gave, but they must not be taken to agree with all or any of what follows. John Comaroff also read the manuscript and made innumerable helpful suggestions; but his contribution goes beyond that as, in the course of a close collaboration on several projects, we have repeatedly discussed many of the questions written about here. Without the help and support of my wife, Marian, I would not have got anywhere with this at all.

Blackheath,   S. R.
14 August 1978

2. 'The Anthropological Study of Law', Nader (ed.), *The Ethnography of Law*, *American Anthropologist*, special supplement to vol. 67 (1965), 3–32.

3. 'The Comparative Study of Dispute Institutions in Society', *Law and Society Review*, vol. 8 (1973), 217–347.

1
Introduction

Although contemporary debates in some western societies reveal an almost obsessive concern with questions of social order, there is very little agreement as to the foundations upon which such order rests or how it can best be secured. Some see it as depending upon widespread approval of mutually understood rules, while others consider that it is primarily maintained through the exercise of force. At the same time, there is argument over the degree of order that is necessary or desirable, and consequently as to the significance of disputes: these can be viewed as pathological events, signs that something is 'wrong' in society; or as normal and inevitable features of social life. Such disagreements are certainly not confined to laymen, and are reflected in the opposition of 'conflict' and 'consensus' theories advanced by professional social scientists.[1]

In this book these and other questions concerning the maintenance of order and the handling of disputes are examined in the different context provided by those less complex societies which social anthropologists have traditionally studied. Small in scale and with relatively simple technologies, few of them have governmental arrangements which we would instantly recognize and a majority entirely lack the centralized state organization with which our own most prominent control institutions are associated. Yet the reports of these societies which became available as Africa, the Americas, Asia and the Pacific were opened up in the course of colonial expansion forced early ethnographers and sociologists of 'primitive law'

1. An introduction to these arguments in contemporary sociology can be gained from the papers collected by Demerath and Peterson in *System, Change and Conflict*.

to rethink some of their most basic ideas about the nature of social order. The accounts showed that far from being the savage anarchies which certain political scientists had postulated (and which earlier, sketchy reports by missionaries, explorers and traders had tended to confirm), these societies were quite orderly and capable of holding together over time. The regularities of behaviour observed in them might sometimes be bizarre and even shocking to the western eye; but it was undeniable that people in them managed to live relatively ordered social lives. This was so even in societies where no 'chiefs' could be found and where the largest political unit consisted of small groups of people united only by ties of kinship. Yet if there were no policemen and prisons, scholars asked, what made people obey the rules? How did disputes ever get settled if there were no judges?

As we shall see when we consider the early literature of legal anthropology,[2] some initial explanations of this unexpected order were not entirely satisfying; but convincing answers were gradually arrived at and a range of control mechanisms identified which made the cohesion of these stateless groupings much less mysterious that it seemed at first. At the same time, this research aided the recognition that similar mechanisms play an important part in securing order in societies like our own, and prompted acceptance of the idea that a large burden of social control must be borne in all societies by extra-legal mechanisms.

The surprise with which reports of viable stateless societies were first greeted draws attention to a problem we shall have to contend with throughout this study: the strength of our native preconceptions and our difficulty in understanding arrangements which cannot be related to our own institutional forms. It was only because of an ethnocentric assumption that order demands the help of centrally organized enforcement agencies that the cohesion of these small-scale societies was initially hard to understand.

The strength and durability of these preconceptions can be

2. See pp. 184–91.

judged from the fact that many scholars have shown a continuing determination to pursue the study of how order is maintained and disputes are settled in these societies within the framework of western legal theory, despite the patent lack of close institutional counterparts to our own arrangements. At first these studies had an openly evolutionary character as people looked to those societies for signs of the foundations upon which our own legal system had grown up. But even when other people's control institutions came to be studied for their own sake, rather than for purposes auxiliary to the understanding of our own system, a strong legal-evolutionary bias often remained. Writers still identified the control institutions they found as 'pre-legal' or 'proto-legal'. At the same time our own arrangements continued to provide the yardstick whereby other people's were categorized as more or less 'advanced'; more or less well suited to the purposes of maintaining order. The very labels which these studies came to be known by – 'primitive law' and subsequently 'legal anthropology' – testify to the strength of this tradition.

Faced with the apparent disparity between the legal systems of contemporary western societies and the control institutions of the societies we shall be studying, it is necessary to begin by asking whether our ideas about law can provide a satisfactory framework for understanding and describing the control mechanisms we find elsewhere. Is our legal theory entirely parochial, or does it constitute a safe base from which to commence cross-cultural studies? This important preliminary question forms the subject of Chapter 2.

Finding that our ideas about law provide an insecure starting point for examining other peoples' institutions of social control, the boundaries of the study must be identified in some other way. In attempting this two simple assumptions are made. First, it is taken for granted here that a degree of order and regularity *must* be maintained in any human group if the basic processes of life are to be sustained. Secondly, it is recognized that quarrels will inevitably arise, and that these may disrupt that order if they are not resolved or at least contained. So the questions are no longer: 'Have they got law?' 'How closely do their legal institutions match our own?' Instead they become: 'How is order maintained?' 'By what means are quarrels dealt with?' Some of the ground surrounding these basic questions is cleared in Chapters 3 and 4.

In looking for the answers to them it is necessary to keep in mind some of the basic resemblances and dissimilarities we are likely to encounter. The common features of these societies are few beyond the fact that they are all relatively small in scale and simple in technology, and that relationships within them are likely to be many-stranded and based on kinship. Limited though these similarities are, they have important implications for the way in which order is maintained. Smallness of scale alone ensures that a dispute arising in connection with one relationship tends to affect others in which the individuals concerned are involved; and the community as a whole is likely to be concerned in a dispute involving any member. The importance of kinship ties in securing order in these societies has been very widely recognized by anthropologists. Turner,[3] for example, notes how closely 'social control at the local level is associated with position in the kinship structure. Senior kin exert authority over and command respect of their juniors, and between each category of kinsmen custom has prescribed an intricate and specific pattern of behavioural expectations which facilitates cooperation and inhibits dispute.'

The differences between these societies range widely, touching upon form of social organization, the manner in which a living is made and the variety of values and beliefs which members hold. Each of these variables may have important implications for the way in which order is maintained and disputes are settled. In pursuing the implications which different means of subsistence may have, we contrast in Chapters 5 and 6 societies of nomadic hunger-gatherers with peoples who make a living through cultivating and stock-herding; and ask what consequences a nomadic existence or a more settled life may have for the manner of social control.

3. *Schism and Continuity in an African Society*, p. 77.

Equally important are variations in social and political organization. Here the societies we consider, in Chapters 7 and 8, range from small acephalous communities made up of nothing more elaborate than groups of undifferentiated kinsmen, through societies with complex lineage and age-set organizations, to those centralized states with rulers and bureaucracies.

Something which appears clearly from the ethnographic material examined in these chapters is that, while a range of control mechanisms contributes to the handling of disputes in any society, the combinations in which such mechanisms are found and their relative importance differ markedly from one place to another. Notably, whereas some form of settlement-directed talking represents a preferred method of dealing with disputes in many societies, fighting is the approved means in others. There also appear to be significant differences in the importance attached to rules in processes of dispute settlement; some peoples seem pedantically rule-bound, others much less preoccupied with normative constraints. Neither kind of variation seems entirely explicable in terms of mode of life or form of social organization; yet both seem closely related to the dominant values held within a particular grouping. Where aggressive self-reliance and loud, vivid responses reflect important values, fighting often constitutes a primary method of resolving disputes. On the other hand, where a 'low profile' and a retiring manner are approved, settlement-directed talk is typically prominent. When we come to look at these questions in Chapters 9 and 10 we shall consider Bohannan's observation that there are 'basically two forms of conflict resolution: administered rules and fighting. Law and war.'[4] Do these stark alternatives portray the matter accurately? If so, upon what does the choice depend?

Up to that point in the book the literature is introduced on a piecemeal basis. We conclude with a more orderly look at the writings of legal anthropology and the main themes they have embraced. This is intended first as a guide to the reader

4. *Law and Warfare*, p. xiii.

who wishes to pursue the subject further than it is taken here. Such help is made necessary by the vigour and diversity of the writing which has followed the path-breaking work of Maine in the mid-nineteenth century.[5] Secondly, in tracing the way in which the subject has developed we can tie together some of the main arguments considered in earlier chapters.

5. *Ancient Law.*

2
Why Not Law?

Whatever view we take about the ultimate basis of order in this society, we are likely to agree as to the important part played by the legal system; either as ensuring compliance with mutually agreed rules, or as a means through which a few members of society manage to exercise power over the rest. But despite the prominence of our legal institutions we must recognize from the beginning that they represent a special feature of one society which will not necessarily be duplicated within any of those we are concerned with here. Furthermore, we should accept the probability that our legal theory will be closely linked to these parochial forms. If that is so, how far can an understanding of the vocabulary, concepts and institutional arrangements which we associate with 'law' be of value when we investigate the ways in which order is maintained elsewhere?

It has come to be recognized as a central problem of the social sciences that in any inquiry the observer is prone to fit the material under investigation, consciously or unconsciously, into a conceptual and institutional framework of his own, distorting the material as he does so. The hazard is obvious where the subject matter he is trying to understand and describe is located in an alien culture; and the risks are perhaps greatest where the arrangements under observation bear a superficial resemblance to those in our own society about which we may have established clear and dogmatic ideas. Anthropologists and philosophers have worried and argued endlessly over the extent to which this hazard may be avoided, and as to the means best employed in attempting to do so.[1] Given that

1. See for example: Winch, 'Understanding a Primitive Society',

complete safety is unattainable but that it is nonetheless desired
to see how order is maintained in another culture, some basic
precautionary steps seem uncontroversial. First, the observer
should try to obtain a clear idea of his own preconceptions,
and constantly remind himself of what these are so they are
not allowed to slip subconsciously into his understanding and
description of other people's arrangements. Secondly, he
should pay close attention to the manner in which people in
the society under observation explain what they do and say.
Lastly, when he subsequently establishes an analytical framework for comparative purposes, he must do his best to see
that this is not seriously coloured by parochial features drawn
from his society or the one he has investigated.

The presence of these risks, and the probable strength of
our preconceptions about law, makes it important to identify
the characteristics of our own legal institutions and examine
the theories which have grown up around them.[2] Once this
has been done, a brief look at the salient features of the
societies we shall be studying will show how inappropriate to
our own purpose is the complex of ideas we have formed
about 'law'. At the same time, this exercise will help us to
guard against the possibility of our domestic preconceptions
creeping into our understanding of other societies by the back
door.

Most lawyers and laymen would probably describe law to
an outsider in terms of legislature, rules, courts and enforcement agencies. Of the legislature it would be noted that while
this body does not constitute the sole source of legal rules
(these may otherwise arise out of custom and be found in the
decisions of judges), it remains the ultimately authoritative

---

American Philosophical Quarterly, vol. I, pp. 307–24; McIntyre, 'Is
understanding religion compatible with believing it?' Hick (ed.), *Faith
and the Philosophers*; Bohannan, *Justice and Judgment among the Tiv*;
Gluckman, 'Reappraisal', *The Judicial Process among the Barotse of
Northern Rhodesia*.

2. The reader who wishes to pursue contemporary British jurisprudence
further should start with Hart's elegant and authoritative work *The
Concept of Law*.

one, capable of altering existing rules and thus of introducing explicit innovations in response to perceived social need.

Among the remaining components, legal rules would be said to have the dual purpose of prescribing approved avenues of conduct for people to follow and of providing criteria whereby disputes can be settled where these arise. A careful description would also emphasize the discrete character of legal rules and the fact that they can be clearly distinguished from those of other normative orders, such as etiquette and morality, both in the manner of their organization and in the way in which they operate. Their source in statutes, the decisions of judges and legal texts makes them readily identifiable and distinguishable as a separate category from other types of norm. So far as the operation of legal rules is concerned, these are seen (at least by lawyers and judges) as being invested with special authority, prescribing courses of conduct which people are obliged to follow if desired results are to be achieved or some wrongful act avoided. In the event of a dispute they are also seen as ultimately authoritative in that they alone determine what the outcome will be.

The subject of legal rules must be linked to that of the courts, the dispute-settlement agencies where they are ultimately applied in the event of a quarrel. Although this might be taken for granted in a lawyer's explanation, it is important for our purposes to note that the courts are specialized in the sense that their sole function is to administer the law in the context of disputes which are brought before them. The impression of specialization is reinforced by the fact that disputes are heard in places not used for other purposes and that unique ceremonial procedures are associated with the process of settlement. Further, the personnel who staff the higher courts, the judges, are generally not allowed to do other jobs at the same time, and are particularly expected to avoid involvement in politics.

It is also important to understand the manner in which the courts are ideally seen to handle disputes which come before them. Each case is dealt with by a judge who listens to both sides and then imposes a decision from a third-party stand-point. It is seen as essential that in fulfilling this umpiring role a judge should act in an impartial manner. The criteria he uses are the legal rules which have already been referred to. Rules derived from other normative systems cannot help him and he is seen as having very little choice as to the rules applicable in the given case; the facts which the disputants bring before him indicate the rules upon which the decision must be based. Thus, the ideal relationship between *rule* and *decision* is clear-cut: the facts lead the judge to the appropriate rule in the repertoire, which in turn indicates the decision: *Rule determines outcome*. Many observers have questioned the accuracy of this model in its applicability to actual instances of judicial behaviour, particularly the relationship which it assumes between rule and decision. In so far as it postulates a lack of discretion on the part of the judge in selecting the rules on which a decision is based, and implies that legal rules form a certain and consistent repertoire of norms, it also seems open to criticism.[3] Nonetheless, it provides the official explanation of the way in which the system works.

One important consequence which flows from such a system of rule-based adjudication is that little element of compromise is encouraged. Once the issue is before the judge he is expected to decide the matter, rather than act as a mediator between the two disputants. While it is possible for him to propose to the parties that they go away and reach a negotiated solution between themselves, most judges seem reluctant to do so, and if the parties reject such a suggestion the judge has no alternative but to hand down his rule-based decision. Also inherent in this method of adjudication is the result that one party wins and the other loses (unless the matter is composite and elements of the decision go in different directions); it is not an objective of the system that both parties should go away

3. For some early and very robust criticisms of the official model, see Frank, *Law and the Modern Mind*.

feeling that they have won, or even that honours have been shared.

Another consequence of this method of dealing with disputes is that once a matter is in the hands of the legal specialists, the lawyers and the judge, they impose their own construction upon it in such a way that both the form and the course which the dispute takes are largely beyond the disputants' control. What is in dispute and how it is to be dealt with are determined by the reach of legal rules. Further, issues which no legal rules can be found to touch are not justiciable, irrespective of any sense of grievance a disputant may feel. A narrow concept of relevance also requires that a precise issue in dispute is separated from any larger complex of relations between the two disputants, and dealt with in isolation from other aspects of their relationship. Such a system can be feasible in large, anonymous communities where many incidents out of which disputes arise provide the only point of contact between those involved, but it can hardly be so where the disputants live in continuing face-to-face relations. It is noticeable that where the judges are explicitly given a broad discretion in resolving disputes arising out of many-stranded relationships (as they are in some types of family disputes), they are less at home than when they have clear-cut rules to fall back on.

A final key characteristic of this system is the presence of official enforcement agencies – bailiffs, the police and the prison service – whose explicit function is to ensure, *by force* if necessary, that legal rules are complied with and to carry out decisions of the courts relating to instances of non-compliance. These agencies, like the courts, are organs of the state.

Several aspects of this familiar picture require emphasis for the present purpose. The first is that important elements of the legal system are directly linked to and dependent upon the particular form of governmental organization established in this society. Part, at least, of the special authority enjoyed by legal rules must be attributable to the ascendency which parliament, the main rule-making body, has acquired. This authority must also be linked to the availability of enforcement agencies to secure compliance with them, itself a feature of the centralized state – as is the presence of a hierarchy of appointed specialists with authority to adjudicate in disputes.

Another characteristic feature is the apparently differentiated character of 'the law' as a discrete sub-system, rather cut off from the rest of society. All this is exemplified in the specialized nature of legal rules and of the courts; the latter being remote places we only visit in the event of a dispute, presided over by specialists who conduct their business against a background of unfamiliar ritual. Even our access to the legal system is typically through further specialists in the form of barristers and solicitors. These latter are themselves distanced from those who seek their services by elaborate training and distinctive habits of work both closely regulated by the professional associations to which they belong (the Law Society and the Inns of Court).

Consistent with all this is the idea in our society that legal and political processes should be kept strictly apart. This notion is given formal expression in the doctrine of 'separation of powers', and the associated prohibition against judicial participation in politics. It is also repeatedly reinforced in official and sentimental utterances of judges and politicians concerning the 'independence' of the judiciary and the sanctity of the law. The extent to which these two areas remain distinct in reality is open to question; but the notion that they should be separate is very deeply entrenched in the ideology.

Alongside the specialized and discrete nature of the legal system it is necessary to emphasize something else we tend to take for granted – the pre-eminent authority of 'the law' in its assigned area of operation. In its sphere it enjoys a position of absolute supremacy: all other normative systems give way to legal rules; and the courts are ultimately the authoritative agencies of dispute settlement. Even though this supremacy is seldom questioned it is jealously guarded and very vigorously defended at the slightest hint of challenge, by the courts themselves as well as by parliament and the executive. For this purpose the courts have available to them the contempt procedures, a main function of which is to stifle alternative modes of dispute settlement. The way these procedures work was illustrated recently when the *Sunday Times* tried to put pressure on the Distillers Company to settle the Thalidomide case by publishing a series of articles on the background to the dispute, in respect of which proceedings before the courts had already been commenced.[4] On that occasion, with the encouragement of the attorney-general, the courts moved swiftly to punish the newspaper for trying to tackle a question which they perceived to be within their exclusive preserve. Whatever the merits of that matter, the case illustrated the speed and the power with which the courts identify and disarm a threatening competitor.

Much of modern English legal theory, predominantly imperative and positivist in character, has been very closely linked to the model just outlined, laying strong emphasis on institutional features such as a rule-making body, the judiciary and enforcement agencies. Almost without exception, the question 'What is law?' has been answered in terms which take for granted some centralized state organization and isolate as essential attributes the presence of rules, courts or sanctions. This view of the legal order appears early in the writings of Hobbes where law is depicted as rules 'commanded' upon the subject by the sovereign.[5] An imperative theory is further developed in the work of Austin where law remains the command of a sovereign directed towards members of the society in a 'habit of obedience', failure to comply being met with 'sanctions'.[6] Other theorists stress the normative and judicial aspects. Salmond, for example, writes of English law as 'nothing

4. *The Thalidomide Children and the Law: A Report by the Sunday Times.* This action on the part of the court was consistent with a long established practice under which alternative modes of dispute settlement must be suspended as soon as a quarrel becomes *sub judice.*

5. *Leviathan*, part 2, Chapter 26.

6. *The Province of Jurisprudence Determined.*

but the body of rules recognized and applied by English courts in the administration of justice'.[7]

While the command theory is now seen to be simplistic and in some respects inaccurate, even the most recent and sophisticated formulations, such as those of Hart,[8] are for the most part developments of it, and remain difficult to apply outside the context of a western legal system. Hart's elucidation of law lays central emphasis on rules. One essential category of these is made up of 'primary rules' imposing obligations. The distinguishing mark of such a rule is the *seriousness* of the pressure to conform to it: 'Rules are conceived and spoken of as imposing obligations when the general demand for conformity is insistent and the social pressure brought to bear upon those who deviate or threaten to deviate is great.'[9] While Hart concedes that a society might exist with primary rules only, they alone do not constitute a legal system. For the step from 'the pre-legal into the legal world' to be made,[10] these primary rules must be supplemented with 'secondary rules' of three kinds: rules of recognition making it possible to identify what the primary rules are; rules of change providing for the alteration of primary rules when the need arises; and rules of adjudication empowering certain people to determine whether on a given occasion the primary rules have been broken. Most systems will also contain other secondary rules authorizing the application of penalties where primary rules are violated; but this further refinement is not seen as essential to a legal system.[11] Through the device of these secondary rules Hart appears to dissociate his model from any parochial institutional content and invest it with considerable value for cross-cultural purposes. But the escape is illusory because the three categories of secondary rules imply, and require, the presence of legislative and adjudicatory agencies. Hart recognizes that this requirement may not be met in all societies, as it is 'possible to imagine a society

7. *Jurisprudence*, p. 113.
8. *The Concept of Law*.
9. ibid., p. 84.
10. ibid., p. 224.
11. ibid., p. 95.

without legislature, courts or officials of any kind', but does not consider that many would in practice be excluded on this account. He states that any community managing with primary rules alone would necessarily be a small one and that 'few societies have existed in which legislative and adjudicative organs and centrally organized sanctions were all entirely lacking'.[12] While there may be some room for argument as to what constitutes legislative and adjudicative organs, or centrally organized sanctions, Hart appears simply wrong upon this last point: many societies *have* existed without them and it is with how order is secured in such societies that we shall be primarily concerned. Furthermore, it is his insistence upon these features which makes his ideas of so little help to us here.

While some of the societies which anthropologists have typically studied do have forms of centralized government, a majority of them are made up of small, face-to-face, acephalous communities which hold together without the apparatus of the state, and in which the control mechanisms which we have so far considered are either entirely absent or at least appear in a considerably modified form. Some of the difficulties of observing such societies through the spectacles of a lawyer appear clearly if we consider that complex of rules, courts and enforcement agencies which we see as central to our own arrangements. Take first the idea of a legal rule. At the root of everyday life in any society there must necessarily be some patterns of habitual conduct followed by the members, providing a basis upon which one member will be able to predict how another is likely to behave under given circumstances and how his own actions will be received. But in some small-scale societies a normative base for these regularities is not clearly conceptualized or articulated; people simply do not always think in terms of rules and obligations. Even where they do, there is almost never found a separate class of 'legal rules', distinguished in function and organiza-

12. ibid., p. 244.

tion from other types of norm in quite the way that this category is within our own society. Norms of polite behaviour,
moral standards and a class of mandatory rules taken most
seriously in the event of a dispute may not be distinguished in
indigenous classifications. Thus, our point of departure in a
clearly defined corpus of legal rules can provide little help in
the study of these groups; nor can we be sure that people in
another culture will think and speak in terms of 'ought' propositions at all.

Obstacles of a similar nature confront cross-cultural use of
our adjudicatory model in the study of dispute settlement. In
almost all societies, including those of nomadic hunters and
gatherers, meeting and talking is seen as a way of resolving
some disputes; but the comparision cannot necessarily be
taken further than that. Even when settlement-directed discussion is an approved and dominant means of resolving a dispute,
it must not be assumed that the mode of settlement employed
in our courts is necessarily followed. In stateless societies,
there may well be no one recognized as competent to hand
down a decision to disputants from a third-party standpoint,
let alone enforce that decision once it has been made. Thus,
third parties are typically limited to acting as go-betweens,
transmitting messages from one disputant to another, or as
mediators, actively coaxing the parties towards a settlement,
but still without the power to resolve the matter by decision.
Even in the case of those relatively few centralized states
where the most 'court-like' institutions have been observed
and adjudicatory procedures are followed, there is seldom
much distinction between legal and political processes or
evidence of the clear relationship between rule and outcome
which is seen ideally to characterize our dispute settlement
process. Most important, perhaps, is the fact that even where
judicial institutions are found they do not always enjoy the
unchallenged pre-eminence in the business of dispute settlement which our courts claim and manage to exercise. Fighting
and other forms of self-help, resort to supernatural agencies,
the use of shaming and ridicule, or the unilateral withdrawal

of essential forms of cooperation may all constitute equally approved and effective means of handling conflict.

The stress which much western legal theory has placed upon organized force and the role of enforcement agencies can also lead to misunderstandings so far as many of these societies are concerned. It has its clearest application in those centralized states which are headed by a ruler with the equivalent of military or police powers at his disposal. Outside a society of this type it may be highly misleading to see force as the ultimate incentive towards compliance with socially accepted rules. In many acephalous communities the most dreaded and effective sanction in the face of sustained antisocial behaviour is *withdrawal* by other members of the society from social contact and the withholding of essential forms of economic cooperation: quite the reverse of what we commonly understand as coercive force.

Underlying these specific obstacles to the cross-cultural use of a 'legal model' the basis for the sharpest contrast between such societies and our own lies in the differentiated character of our legal arrangements, existing as they do as a discrete and specialized sub-system having to do exclusively with matters which we identify as 'legal'. Despite the wide range of organizational forms which may be found in small-scale societies, the mechanisms for maintaining continuity and handling disputes tend almost universally to be directly embedded in everyday life, unsupported by a differentiated legal system. Even in the large Central and Southern African kingdoms, with governmental institutions superficially like our own, clear isolation of legal institutions is not entirely duplicated.[13]

Given this lack of 'fit' between our own legal arrangements and the control mechanisms in the societies we shall be considering, and the consequent inapplicability of much of our legal theory, it seems best to avoid centring the discussion upon law altogether. Were we to insist upon doing so, the

13. See Chapter 8 below.

term 'law' would either have to be used excessively loosely, or else we would need to exclude from consideration control mechanisms which in many societies hold central importance.

Under these circumstances it becomes necessary to establish a different framework for this study; one that will not come under strain in the face of diverse values and various institutional forms. In choosing to focus on 'order' and 'dispute', two simple assumptions are made. First I take for granted that some degree of regularity must prevail in any social group if it is to survive. That much is implied in the very idea of a society. Secondly, it is assumed that disputes are inevitable; as Weber insisted: 'conflict cannot be excluded from social life'.[14] No originality is claimed for this broad perspective. Malinowski implied the necessity of adopting it when he wrote: 'In such primitive communities I personally believe that law ought to be defined by function and not by form, that is we ought to see what are the arrangements, the sociological realities, the cultural mechanisms which act for the enforcement of law.'[15] The same approach is suggested in the concern of some American 'realist' theory with what law *does* rather than what it *is*.[16]

Against this line of attack it can be argued that to follow it casts the net very wide, causing the rigour of analysis to be lost. The chunk of social life marked out for examination becomes too large to control. The dangers of attempting so broad a field must be acknowledged; so must the advantages of a narrower one which would confine comparative study to rules which are taken seriously, to centrally organized sanctions and to court-like institutions. But for our purposes the difficulty with the narrower approach is that it involves giving emphasis to distinctions which can have no meaning in many of the societies we shall be considering. It could therefore only prove artifici-

14. *The Methodology of the Social Sciences*, trans. Shils and Finch, p. 26.

15. Introduction to Hogbin, *Law and Order in Polynesia*, p. lxiii.

16. See, for example, Llewellyn and Hoebel's formulation of the 'law jobs' theory in *The Cheyenne Way*, Chapter 11.

ally constricting and at the same time encourage us to see other people's control institutions in the potentially distorting light of our own.

3

Order and Continuity in Everyday Life

Some degree of order and regularity must be assured if social life in any community is to be sustained. This state need not be one of quiet harmony, and indeed societies differ widely as to the amount of friction and disorder which their members seem able to tolerate; but conditions must be such that children can be reared and consistent arrangements made for the provision of food, drink and shelter. If this is to be achieved an element of order must endure over time within the group as well as between that group and any other with which it is in immediate contact. In this chapter we consider what foundations the first, internal, aspect of order rests on; what it consists of and how its continuity is secured.

It should be recognized from the start that the conditions we are talking about need not be associated with any particular form of governmental organization. The prerequisites for survival certainly do not include the presence of a ruler, able to keep the peace by force among his people. As we have already noted, many of the societies we shall be considering are acephalous, without centralized government and agencies expressly concerned with the enforcement of order. But even in societies where such arrangements are present there is room for argument as to their importance in holding everything together. Indeed, scholars disagree profoundly as to whether the cohesion of a society like our own is primarily attributable to the presence of mutually accepted rules or to the coercive exercise of power.[1] At first sight there is little room for such debate in societies without explicit enforcement agencies, but even in the absence of a ruler, coercive elements may still be present (if superficially

1. See footnote 1 on p. 11 above.

concealed) in an age-set organization or kinship system which entrenches the dominance of elderly or genealogically senior men.

Whatever the particular balance between consensus and coercion in securing compliance, order in any society must depend first upon some understanding existing among the members as to how the activities of everyday life shall be arranged, and as to what are to be acceptable and unacceptable forms of conduct in a given context. In the absence of such shared assumptions, enabling A to predict how B should behave in familiar circumstances and how A's own actions ought to be received, social life could scarcely exist. Similarly, there must be conventions concerning response to the new and unexpected; readily understood signals telling A how B is reacting to something unfamiliar. How much is provided for in a basic pool of mutually understood norms, and how much is left over for discussion and adjustment as life goes along, must depend in part on the size and closeness of the community concerned. We shall see in a later chapter that in very small groups where all the members can speak freely to each other, and are thus in a position to know most of the time what each is thinking and doing, the very sparsest rule-base is possible, with much being left to specific understanding and agreement as the need arises.[2] But even in the tiniest unit it would scarcely be feasible for an individual to act on all occasions in accordance with a plan expressly agreed in advance with all the other members; such a way of life would be intolerably laborious, even if in the short term it might be achieved.

What these shared understandings are, and the range of matters to which they relate, will depend upon the values and beliefs held by members of the society concerned, their ways of making a living and their modes of social organization. At the very least there must be socially accepted norms regulating inter-personal violence, as well as some provision for sexual access, the sharing of food, and the management of other scarce and valued resources. In a group of nomadic hunters and

2. See p. 82 below.

gatherers a narrow and meagre rule-base may be sufficient, whereas in societies where land is cultivated and cattle are kept there must be, out of necessity, a much wider range of matters subject to accepted patterns of conduct. At the same time the more elaborate the form of social organization, the bulkier the rule-base will become.

Although in any society understandings shared by the members must underlie many of the regularities of behaviour which can be observed, human groups vary a great deal in the extent to which these understandings are translated into explicit rules which members talk about. Some peoples talk freely about their rules, quote them constantly in everyday life, and furnish detailed inventories for anyone who may ask about them. Others find it difficult to think and speak in terms of rules (i.e. in terms of how people 'ought' to behave) at all.[3] But it does not follow that because people do not talk about rules they are unimportant. Norms of fundamental importance may be accepted tacitly and rest implicit in the basic organizational features of a society: how relationships are traced; the groupings within which people live; who they do and do not marry; and the directions in which office or property devolve.

Furthermore, although in any community individuals may be expected to go about ordering their affairs in what they conceive to be their best interests, the extent to which compliance with rule is stressed in this process is variable. In some societies such compliance is strongly emphasized in the ideology, and explicitly seen as the only means whereby the society will hold together. Elsewhere everyday behaviour is judged much more in terms of what others will tolerate in a given situation, of how particular interests may best be achieved, and of what may be gained or lost through a particular transaction. Some people more than others may thus follow what one anthropologist has described as a 'manipulative, bargaining, transactional approach to life'.[4] Even where rules are spelled out, there may

3. See p. 170 below.
4. Stanner, 'Continuity and Schism in an African Tribe – A review', *Oceania*, vol. 29, 205, p. 208.

be different attitudes towards their breach; in some groups the successful and highly esteemed man is the one who flouts normally accepted rules and patterns of conduct. It may be understood that the 'big men' will break the rules, and that their ascendancy lies in doing so.

In this context it is important to remember that societies differ widely as to the kinds of behaviour which are approved or tolerated and hence also in the amount of tension and quarrelling that will be felt acceptable. The possibilities can be seen as ranged along a continuum. At one end are societies in which subdued, self-effacing conduct is expected of the members. Here, peace and quiet and sustained harmonious inter-personal relations represent dominant values, and urgent appeals for unity are made wherever a quarrel shows signs of developing. An example of such a society is provided by the North American Zuni Indians. Among them quarrelling is strongly disapproved, and a man is expected to avoid any form of controversy or conspicuous behaviour. We shall consider later a similar example in the Mbuti, a group of nomadic hunters and gatherers living in the tropical forests of the Congo.[5] Elsewhere, at the opposite end of the scale, loud, aggressive behaviour may be approved and a high value attached to individual ascendancy and achievement. In such a society it may be 'by asserting himself against others, making them do what he wants or doing what he wants with them, that a man shows himself to be "strong" '.[6] There, persistent disputes may be tolerated, ignored or even enjoyed. While in one society peace and quiet may be prized above everything, elsewhere people may openly relish a quarrel. Such accounts confirm that attitudes towards trouble vary greatly from one place to another according to the values of the group concerned, and that conflict is by no means seen universally as unhealthy or to be avoided.

Thus far, it should be clear that whatever the shared assumptions against which everyday life in a particular society may go on, we should not start out with the idea that peace and

---

5. See p. 94 below.
6. Berndt, *Excess and Restraint*, p. 398.

harmony necessarily represent a 'natural' state of things, disrupted only by occasional, pathological instances of trouble. Further, it would appear that in most societies, if not in all, some degree of disharmony is rendered inevitable by the very beliefs which the members hold. There are, for example, widely encountered beliefs that ill-health, death and other misfortunes may result where unfriendly human beings seek to cause harm to others through sorcery or by invoking the help of supernatural agencies. Where such ideas are present, each incident is a potential source of conflict, and however firmly suspicions associated with it may be laid to rest, someone else will fall ill or die, setting off another round of trouble.

Trouble may also be inherent in the most basic features of a society's organization. Here the Ndembu of Zambia provide an illustration which we will have to consider again later.[7] Among them, while the headmanship of a village may be confined to a group of matrilineal kinsmen, there are no rules identifying which particular person should succeed, with the result that individual members of the lineage are left to compete among themselves for the headmanship. Bitter quarrels typify this competition, and while these die down once a new headman is established, they inevitably flare up again as he grows old and loses his grip on the community. Thus in some societies at least, order and regularity are best seen as secured against a background of conflict, some forms of which are inherent in the very beliefs and systems of organization, and hence sure to recur again and again however successfully individual 'incidents' may be handled and smoothed over.

Whatever the values subscribed to in a society, and the attendant repertoire of socially accepted norms, these are passed on to members of each successive generation as they mature. This process, a matter of learning how to adjust behaviour and expectations in relation to others toward whom you stand in differing social relations, is part of the business

7. Turner, *Schism and Continuity in an African Society*; see also pp. 46–7 below.

of growing up in any group. Partly this involves simply being around and seeing what is done and not done; and what attracts approval and what displeasure. Partly it is a matter of the 'right' forms of behaviour being expressly taught. The exact balance of these two sources in the overall process of socialization varies very much from one society to another. In some cases elaborate initiation periods, during which explicit instruction is given into the approved ways of the group, precede admission to adult status. In the course of these processes of initiation express verbal warnings and instructions may be given and repeated over and over again; plays may be enacted depicting the consequences of approved and disapproved forms of conduct. In others, little explicit attention is given to preparing young people for life in the community; they are left to pick this up by observation and experience.

The process of socialization does not end with the transition to adult status, however that may be achieved, but continues through every stage of life. In identifying the ways in which this continual process is sustained, anthropologists have repeatedly emphasized the importance of ceremonial and ritual procedures. These procedures, whether associated with irregular crises in the human cycle such as birth, marriage and death, or with fixed points in the calendar, are widely interpreted as reinforcing and affirming established values. Thus, the elaborate ceremonial and feasting which widely attends such crises as marriage or the devolution of political office from one holder to another may be seen as smoothing the path through these difficult transitions. In the same way, the recurring seasonal festivals in which members of a community may gather together can be seen as cementing the unity of the group and as perpetuating a necessary sense of continuity.

Given the operation of socialization processes, and the reinforcing effects of ritual, how far does compliance with socially approved patterns of behaviour have to be enforced by further control mechanisms? As we have noted, this question preoccupied early observers of 'primitive' communities consider-

ably. In so far as these scholars had thought about the
maintenance of order in their own societies, this had generally
been within the framework of contemporary legal theory.
Among English legal scholars, at least, order was seen at the
end of the nineteenth century in accordance with imperative
theory as being secured through the 'command' of a sovereign
who was capable of enforcing any failure to comply with
'sanctions'. Here, however, were societies with no sign of
governmental institutions as a lawyer would understand them,
but nonetheless order somehow prevailed. How did they hold
together? By the 1920s two competing views of order in
'primitive' societies were current. The earlier of these held
that members of these societies complied unthinkingly like
automata, bound by their customs simply because they were
there, and of long standing. The later one, put forward in
slightly different forms by the anthropologists Radcliffe-Brown
and Malinowski, insisted that in no society was compliance
with accepted norms automatic and that everywhere people
had to be kept in line, although the means whereby this was
achieved differed considerably from place to place. Radcliffe-
Brown argued that in any society certain forms of conduct
were 'sanctioned' in the sense that they were subject to approval (positive sanctions) or disapproval (negative sanctions).[8]
Such approval or disapproval might be expressed in many
different ways, but sanctions were in the first instance effective
'through the desire of the individual to obtain the approbation
and to avoid the disapprobation of his fellows, to win such
rewards and to avoid such punishment as the community
offers or threatens'.[9] Malinowski became dissatisfied with the
earlier theory in the course of his field work in the Trobriand
Islands. As a result of his observations he concluded, in much
the same way, that there was in any society the problem of
curbing 'human inclinations, passions or instinctive drives' and
of protecting 'the rights of one citizen against the con-

8. 'Social Sanctions', *Encyclopaedia of the Social Sciences*, vol. 13,
531–4.
9. ibid., p. 532.

cupiscence, cupidity or malice of the other'. Where this could not be achieved through 'courts and constables', it had to be achieved through other means; everywhere rules needed to be 'baited with inducements'.[10]

Malinowski's argument is attractive and, as we shall see, he supported it vividly with the results of his own field observations; but in implying that men are constantly and strongly inclined to break the rules he over-states his case. Much of the time people *do* comply with established rules without prompting and without thinking; a particular way of doing things has been followed again and again, and with repetition has acquired a 'rightness' over time. This rightness may derive in part simply from the fact that the particular course of conduct has been frequently repeated; but it is likely also to be due to the conduct having acquired a moral quality (i.e. being seen as 'good'), or to its proven efficacy as a 'safe, known routine'.[11] Further, rules are to some extent self-enforcing in that they do not stand alone, inviting a direct choice between compliance and non-compliance, but are linked together and embedded in the overall structure of the society concerned. Where you live, whom you show respect to, whom you marry, which cattle you slaughter; the answers to these questions are implied in what you have done before and in the overall organization of the society in which you live. As one writer has put it, 'In all societies some of the burden of social control, and in some societies nearly all, is permeated through the constant requirements of such things as respect to elders, and the appropriate polite behaviour required by others. Most of the time indeed, this appears to the actors as the only natural way to behave.'[12]

While in much of everyday life compliance may thus be more or less unconscious and without question, at other times

10. Introduction to Hogbin, *Law and Order in Polynesia*, pp. lxii, lxv.
11. Nadel, 'Social Control and Self-Regulation', *Social Forces*, 265, p. 266.
12. Introduction to Bloch (ed.), *Political Language and Oratory in Traditional Society*, pp. 3–4.

immediate personal advantage will be seen to conflict with socially approved rules, or at least with the perceived interests of some other person, requiring the merits and hazards of a particular course of conduct to be carefully weighed. At such a moment, among the various strands which motivate personal action, an assessment of *how other people will react* assumes central importance. The immediate advantage then has to be weighed against the likely upshot of other people's disapproval: particularly that of those with whom the actor is in close contact and upon whom he will have to rely in future. This disapproval may be translated into ridicule, loss of prestige, physical retaliation, appeal to third parties for some kind of intervention, resort to sorcery, the withdrawal of valued cooperation, or even total ostracism. As will be shown in the following chapters, the actor's appreciation of these possibilities and the fear which this appreciation generates may constitute an important mechanism for securing compliance with the socially accepted rule.

Among these inducements to follow approved forms of conduct, Malinowski singled out as particularly important for the Trobriand Islanders he studied the threatened withdrawal of valued economic cooperation.[13] In this Melanesian society he noted that each member was bound to others in a complex of reciprocal economic obligations in such a way that persistent failure to honour any particular one could lead to the total collapse of his livelihood. Malinowski saw in this complex of obligations a powerful mechanism for ensuring compliance with the approved norms of Trobriand life. Among these relationships the simplest strand bound together the group of fishermen who shared a boat on the lagoon. These men each carried out a particular task in manning the boat and the net, and through its performance acquired a right to share in the catch. Repeated failure to accompany the fishing expeditions of 'his' boat would deprive a man of his share of the fish. Another strand linked together the fisherman on the lagoon and an inland partner, the yam grower. (Both fish and yams were staples of the Trobriand diet.) The fisherman supplied

13. *Crime and Custom in Savage Society*, pp. 22–32.

the inland farmer with fish, and the farmer the fisherman with yams. If either party persistently failed to honour his side of the arrangement, he would soon find himself without an essential element in his overall resources: no fish, no yams. Malinowski suggested that while such a breakdown could possibly be endured for a while, it would over time have a destructive effect on other relationships, so that in the end the recalcitrant partner would be forced back into line or obliged to live elsewhere. One of the other relationships which could be directly affected was that between husband and wife. In Trobriand society, instead of a man being responsible for feeding his own household – his wife and children – his efforts are directed towards providing for his sister and her husband, while his own needs in this respect are met by his wife's brother. It is not hard to see how the breakdown of any one of these relationships will immediately place the remaining strands in jeopardy. Under such circumstances the mechanism of enforcement lies within the complex of relationships itself, and no external sanction is necessary. In most instances anyone tempted to deviate from approved norms of conduct will check himself; a process labelled by one writer as 'self-regulation'.[14] Perceiving the disadvantages inherent in the proposed behaviour, he will desist without prompting from other people. It is understandable, therefore, that while Malinowski postulated the cohesive force of these relationships of reciprocal obligation, he was not able to give examples of confrontations in which people were obliged to abandon socially disapproved courses of conduct; given the way in which these relationships operated such occasions would seldom arise. Nonetheless, Hogbin, doing research on communities of Polynesian fishermen, has provided case histories of lazy fishermen being forced back to the boats when their idleness gave rise to the withdrawal of essential forms of cooperation upon which they themselves relied.[15]

Malinowski has sometimes been criticized for over-

14. Nadel, 'Social Control and Self-Regulation', *Social Forces*, 265.
15. *Law and Order in Polynesia*, pp. 125–7.

emphasizing the importance of these relationships in holding Trobriand society together. It is certainly doubtful whether such a complex of relationships could provide the exclusive mechanisms for maintaining order in any group; but equally, reciprocal obligations of this kind play an important part in regulating conduct in most societies. Nor do the responsibilities need to be so explicitly defined as they are in the Trobriand case. They can be found in some form or another in almost any community. Consider for a moment a society made up of groups of patrilineal kinsmen, whose norms prohibit marriage within the group to which a man belongs. Even assuming he is tempted to marry a girl within the prohibited degrees, the very manner in which the group is organized will discourage him. His kin will be reluctant to help him with the necessary bridewealth, and it will be clear to him in advance that the valued affinal ties associated with the appropriate 'marriage out' will not materialize. Thus, even if no-one is prompted to take positive action against him, the difficulties presented by the proposed deviation will be formidable.

Even beyond cases of mutual reliance, concern for 'what other people think' seems in most societies to have a powerful influence upon conduct. Numerous reports stress how sensitive people are to ridicule and even the mildest criticism, and go on to assert that this sensitivity influences them strongly in adhering to approved patterns of behaviour. Such reports are not confined to any particular geographical area or type of society. While one anthropologist writes how !Kung Bushmen in the Kalahari 'cannot bear the sense of rejection which even the mildest disapproval makes them feel',[16] others note shame as representing an equally powerful means through which deviant conduct can be controlled in Melanesian communities.[17] In any small closely knit community where people find themselves in continuing face-to-face relations the threat of

16. Marshall, 'Sharing, Talking and Giving: Relief of Social Tension among !Kung Bushmen', *Africa*, vol. 31, 231.

17. See, for example, Hogbin, 'Shame: Social Conformity in a New Guinea Village', *Oceania*, vol. 17, 4.

exposure to ridicule or disgust, provoking feelings of shame and remorse, must represent an important mechanism of control.

So far, in considering fear of shame and loss of valued co-operation we have been concerned with rather negative inducements towards approved behaviour. But the threat of direct personal violence may operate in the same way. Writing about the Nuer, among whom insults and many other wrongs demand immediate retaliation if honour is to be satisfied, Evans-Pritchard asserts that it is the knowledge that a Nuer will 'enforce his rights by club and spear that ensures respect for person and property'.[18] In many stateless societies self-help is not so readily approved as it is among the Nuer; but in most the threat of it retains considerable importance in ensuring compliance with approved patterns of behaviour. In the relatively few centralized states that we are concerned with, the ruler typically claims a monopoly of approved violence, achieving order at least in part through direct 'policing' activities and through the indirect threat presented by knowledge of the enforcement procedures which will be carried out where disapproved conduct is discovered and the culprit caught. But even in these cases enforcement agencies are seldom as specialized as those found in contemporary western societies, and are unlikely to enjoy quite the monopoly of approved force that our enforcement agencies enjoy.

In a society where sorcery is practised and where serious misfortune may be attributed to such action, fear of this mode of attack may play just as important a part in controlling conduct as does the anticipation of direct interpersonal violence elsewhere. Malinowski explicitly identified fear of sorcery as having the effect of inducing behaviour in accordance with approved norms in the Trobriands, and others have followed him in this;[19] but anthropologists are certainly not unanimous in regarding such fear as having a direct controlling influence on behaviour. Here much must depend on

18. *The Nuer*, p. 171.
19. See, for example, Young, *Fighting with Food*, pp. 127–33.

the beliefs entertained in a given society, particularly as to whether sorcery is normally resorted to in response to wrongs.

Alongside the expected reaction of other humans to a particular course of conduct, many reports suggest that sensitivity towards the possible reaction of supernatural beings may have a like effect in shaping behaviour. To most of us the idea that human action might be influenced by fear of attracting God's wrath is familiar. Nonetheless systems of belief seem to differ very markedly in the extent to which supernatural beings are thought to be interested in, or likely to act on the basis of, incidents in everyday human life. In some the possibility of divine intervention in daily matters is disregarded, whereas in others such intervention is considered ubiquitous. As we shall see later, most accounts of Eskimo communities suggest that for them life is hedged about with fear of supernatural action which can be prompted even by the least infringement of detailed dietary rules. Such burdensome beliefs may not be typical, but the idea that disapproved forms of conduct can lead to action on the part of supernatural beings is very widespread indeed. In the case of the Central African Mbuti we shall see that 'noise' is believed to anger the 'forest' who may then bring suffering to the community.[20] Again, the idea that the spirits of the ancestors can be displeased by quarrelling among those on earth, and respond by causing sickness, seems very common. However, while it is easy enough to collect idealized statements as to the controlling influence which fear of the supernatural may have on human conduct, its actual effects are as hard to measure in practice as any other determinant of behaviour.

Examples of all these control mechanisms appear in later chapters; but before we go any further there is one other general point that should be kept in mind. Almost all these means of maintaining order, particularly those which derive their force from the actor's perception of how other people may react, operate through human communication in the

20. See p. 94.

course of everyday life. Through talk, values and norms may be expressly stated, and consequences of departure from them spelled out. Through word, gesture and expression potentially disruptive conduct may be prevented or diverted and warnings conveyed. Such warnings may take very different forms. They may be spelled out explicitly, particularly where there is someone in the group recognized as having authority to do this. Otherwise, the warnings may be indirect; people may speak loudly in disapproval of threatened anti-social behaviour, ostensibly among themselves, but to their knowledge within earshot of the person whose conduct is the subject of discussion. Alternatively, abstract talk about approved norms may be timed and angled in such a way that a warning is given to someone potentially in breach. Where, for example, A is believed to have designs on B's chickens, C and D may sit around in the meeting place speaking with feeling on the evils of stealing in general. Similarly, a serious warning may be dressed up in jests and mockery in such a way that an individual is discouraged from a socially divisive course of conduct without the risk of matters being made worse in a direct confrontation. On a more general level, in any small close-knit community everyone is likely to know through meeting and talking what other people have been doing, who can be relied on, who is to be mistrusted. Under these circumstances, each will know that the attitude of others towards him will depend on his reputation, and fear of adverse report and gossip will encourage him to adjust his conduct accordingly.[21]

The importance of verbal communication concerning approved or disapproved patterns of behaviour is emphasized under conditions of change where novel situations develop, causing established procedures to break down and innovatory conduct to be attempted. It is on such occasions that existing values and norms are likely to be articulated and, in the course of debate, consciously or unconsciously reformulated to accommodate the situation which has arisen.

21. Gluckman, 'Gossip and Scandal', *Current Anthropology*, vol. 4, 307–16.

We should also remember that it is often through talking that one person has the opportunity to control the conduct of another. Because of this, mastery of the approved conventions of speech represents an important skill in almost any society. Such conventions lay down what may be said in given circumstances, how it may be said, and to whom it may be said. By virtue of its enormous range and flexibility, the control implications of speech must everywhere be significant, and some scholars are now urging that studies of order in any society should begin with detailed examination of speech forms, both within and outside the context of dispute. In this connection, recent research has revealed the importance which selective use of different speech patterns may have from the standpoint of social control.[22] Where, for example, a highly formalized code is available and adopted by a speaker, it has been argued that the range of acceptable responses is necessarily reduced, thus increasing the potential for coercion, so long as those involved in the exchange are prepared to remain within the restricted speech conventions concerned.

22. See Bloch (ed.), *Political Language and Oratory in Traditional Society*.

4
Disputes

Disputes, both within groups and between them, are found everywhere in human society. But beyond that generalization social theorists differ profoundly over their nature and significance. Despite the universal occurrence of disputes, some see them as predominantly destructive in character, indicating a breakdown of normal relations and providing a sign that something is 'wrong' in the society where they occur. Others have denied this pathological quality, seeing disputes as an integral and inevitable part of life in any community. Those who have stressed the normality and inevitability of disputes have also paid more attention to their *constructive* attributes than their *negative* ones. At the beginning of his celebrated essay entitled *Conflict*,[1] the German sociologist Georg Simmel suggested that 'there probably exists no social unit in which convergent and divergent currents among its members are not inseparably interwoven', and went on to argue that even if an absolutely harmonious group could be conceived in theory it 'could show no real life process'.[2] Both in his association of conflict with the normal and inevitable in social life, and in his insistence on its necessary and constructive side, Simmel has been widely followed by other sociologists.

Much of the material which we shall be considering certainly confirms that disputes should not necessarily be seen as pathological phenomena arising out of abnormal behaviour, or as indicating some malfunction in the community where

1. 'Der Streit' was originally published as Chapter 4 of Simmel's *Sociologie* (1908). The references here are to the English translation by Wolff, *Conflict*.

2. *Conflict*, p. 15.

they are found. Some forms of conflict are simply inherent in, and rendered inevitable by, the beliefs which members of a society hold as to the nature of the universe and the causes underlying illness, death and material misfortune. If, as we have already noted to be the case in some societies, such crises are believed to result from the reactions of supernatural beings to human conduct which has displeased them, every illness or failure in the food supply will be the potential source of a quarrel as culprits are sought and blame allocated. In Eskimo communities, for example, where certain spirit beings are believed to inflict ill-health when humans have angered them, epidemics are widely reported to constitute a serious source of conflict (see p. 95 below). Equally widely held are the beliefs which attribute illness and material misfortune to the practice of sorcery by ill-disposed neighbours or kinsmen. Where this is the case, any incident leads at once to the suspicion that someone in the community is badly disposed to the sufferer. Attempts at detection then follow; and trouble is an all too likely result, whether a culprit is unambiguously identified or not. Moreover, this source of trouble will remain so long as the relevant beliefs are held, with each successive case of sickness or material loss triggering off another quarrel. Thus the shared beliefs which supply the unifying strands in such a society at the same time constitute an inevitable source of quarrels.

Certain types of conflict may also be inherent in the very manner in which a society is organized. In Chapter 3 we saw how, in the case of the Ndembu, succession to the headmanship of each of the numerous villages of which this society is composed is confined to the males of a particular matrilineage, but beyond that the rules do not demand a specific genealogical connection between one headman and the man who succeeds him; that is determined by individual achievement and prestige. Thus, the most influential males of the dominant lineage compete among themselves for the political leadership, and this process is attended by bitter quarrels. As Turner argues, in such a society the whole developmental cycle of a village community becomes closely linked to the rhythm of disputes generated in the course of struggles for the leadership. As one headman's authority begins to decline the struggles among his potential successors intensify and this process may be traced through the numerous disputes which mark this struggle. When a new leader is established one or more of his competitors may break away with their followers and form new villages elsewhere. Once this has happened, relative calm returns to the community for a time, but the trouble begins again as each successive contest develops. Many other studies identify similar characteristic types of trouble, built into the organization of a community in such a way that they recur inevitably as life goes on.

Simmel's point about the constructive quality of conflict is also illustrated in this Ndembu example. For the struggle for village headship, while disrupting the established unit, at the same time provides a crucial element in the cycle through which existing social forms are reproduced. But even beyond such a case Simmel argues that any conflict is constructive in the sense that its outcome brings with it a re-ordering of previous relations – even a conflict which has resulted in the destruction of one of the parties to it.

It has also been argued that conflict may be constructive in another sense; as having an integrative quality. Where two groups are involved in a quarrel, the members of each faction are likely to be drawn together through their shared antagonism towards the other. We consider the validity of this suggestion later, in the context of warfare between neighbouring groups of the same ethnic affiliation encountered in New Guinea Highland societies.[3]

It must be recognized too that there need be no incompatibility between the idea that disputes have a constructive character and the view that they can originate in the malfunction of existing social institutions. While some quarrels undoubtedly occur in the course of cyclical processes like those taking place in the Ndembu example, others may equally

3. See p. 160 below.

arise out of innovative behaviour, the development of new technologies or changes in the ecology which cannot be accommodated within established social forms. As I suggested in Chapter 3, the debates and disputes generated by such events may provide the context in which novel practices acquire acceptance and in which the values and norms of the group concerned can be expressly articulated or reformulated in a manner compatible with contemporary conditions.

Whatever ideas may be held as to the nature and meaning of disputes, the ostensible issues about which people quarrel must depend largely upon the beliefs that are held, the values subscribed to and the forms of organization prevailing in the society concerned. Much will also depend on how the members go about making a living, as this will determine what there is, in material terms, to quarrel about. Within a group of nomadic hunter-gatherers there may be little beyond questions of sexual access and the distribution of consumer perishables; whereas in other kinds of society tracts of scarce land, hoards of grain and large herds of stock may set the scene for significant quarrels over property.

A. CATEGORIES OF DISPUTE

Any attempt to classify disputes is made difficult at the outset by the diverse forms of human interaction to which the very label 'dispute' may be taken to refer. The range of matters about which people may quarrel is almost infinite, as are the conceivable variations in scale and duration. When we speak of a dispute we may equally contemplate a domestic 'row' which is amicably settled without going further than the spouses immediately involved, or a confrontation between nation states which is ultimately resolved through warfare. Similarly, the term may refer as well to an altercation which arises and is settled in the course of an afternoon as to a feud which lingers on over several generations. Further, there are problems as to the relationship between cause and form. The immediate focus of a quarrel may have little bearing upon the underlying causes of a dispute.

Despite these variations in form, scale and focus, two broad distinctions have often recurred in attempts to classify disputes. One of these has involved contrasting disputes between groups and disputes within a group: inter-group conflict and intra-group conflict. The other has involved an opposition between disputes arising out of broken rules and those having their origin in competition over scarce and valued resources. Something more must be said about both of these distinctions.

i. Disputes between groups and disputes within them

At first sight there is good sense, as well as tempting neatness, in distinguishing disputes between two groups from those which arise between individuals or are at least confined within a single group. But this distinction may prove difficult to maintain because in many of the societies we shall be considering almost *any* dispute necessarily becomes one involving two groups on account of the obligation to rally behind a kinsman which members recognize in the event of trouble. Evans-Pritchard has documented such obligations vividly in the case of the Nuer.[4] There, patrilineal descent is one of the main organizing principles, and when any Nuer tribesman is wronged by another he can expect members of his lineage to support him in exacting revenge against the wrongdoer. Correspondingly, the wrongdoer's co-lineage members will rally round to protect him (and themselves) against such attacks. Similar obligations of support arising out of kinship (some extending to retaliatory violence, others to support of a less active nature) are very widely reported. Even within a particular kinship grouping, principles are sometimes found which indicate to the members which co-member they should support in the event of a quarrel.[5] However far this support extends, and whatever the form of kinship organization through which it is recruited, its existence ensures that other members of the groups concerned are drawn into a dispute.

In other cases third parties may become involved in disputes

4. *The Nuer*, see also pp. 120–21 below.
5. See, for example, the Arusha patrilineage described by Gulliver in *Social Control in an African Society*; see also pp. 132–3 below.

because prior cooperation with the disputants has brought them into relationships of reciprocal obligation. Gulliver describes how such obligations may arise in the case of the Ndendeuli of Southern Tanzania.[6] The Ndendeuli live in small groups of undifferentiated kinsmen in woodland areas where poor soil necessitates a move to fresh fields every two or three seasons. Although they practise a very simple slash-and-burn technique of agriculture, the members of a household require the help of others if their fields are to be cleared, hoed and planted. For this purpose, the head of a household forms a clearing party, calling upon those he has himself helped in the past and will be helping in the future. Over time these arrangements develop into more generalized relationships of reciprocal obligation, involving an expectation of mutual aid outside this narrow economic sphere. This includes the expectation of help when one partner enters into a dispute. When a man gets involved in a quarrel, he will expect to be able to call on the support of those with whom he has cooperated most closely in the past, and in turn he will assume that he will support them in their disputes. Thus, whenever a quarrel arises in an Ndendeuli community, support groups made up of other members will be ranged behind those between whom the trouble originated.

Even where involvement is not demanded by ties of kinship or reciprocal obligation, the nature and size of the group concerned will often ensure that third parties become embroiled. In any small face-to-face community trouble originating between two individuals must come swiftly to the attention of other members. Once it has done so it will be difficult for them to ignore it, as the essential tasks of making a livelihood are likely to be disturbed so long as it continues. Thus, others will be prompted to intervene simply to limit the damage and get people back to the business of making a living again; and in doing so a partisan involvement may be hard to avoid. Such involvement carries the further implication that a quarrel may endure beyond the lifetime of the original disputants. Particu-

6. *Neighbours and Networks.*

larly where groups of kin become opposed, feuds may develop which continue from one generation to another, surviving long after those initially involved in the quarrel are dead.

Whatever the range of people involved in a dispute within a small face-to-face group, it is unlikely that it will disappear without trace, leaving no lasting mark on the community. Those concerned will continue to live at close quarters, participating in the same complex of relationships as existed before the dispute occurred. It will be rare in such a context for trouble to arise out of a single-stranded relationship of the kind that is possible in our society, where disputants may have no further contact with each other after the immediate issues have been resolved. Existing loyalties and hostilities will be tested in the context of each successive dispute, and each one will be closely related to those which precede and follow it, and through them the relationships of people within the community will gradually change over time.

Even when we compare disputes arising between two completely autonomous social groups, and those between subgroups of a single society, the differences observable are not altogether clear-cut. At some levels a distinction may certainly be maintained. In the former case, for example, the resolution of a dispute may be hampered by the absence of shared values and socially accepted rules which would be common to those involved in an internal dispute. Further, the possibility of effective third-party intervention may well be greater in the case of a municipal dispute. Nonetheless, relations between individual communities within a single society, which include sustained fighting in the event of a dispute, and correspond very closely to those between nation states, have been reported from a number of societies.[7]

ii. Broken rules and conflicting interests

As we saw earlier in the present chapter, when we considered Ndembu leadership struggles, conflict need not be associated with 'broken rules'; it may be inherent in the normal operation

7. See pp. 116–20 below.

of the system and generated through approved patterns of behaviour. Examples of such disputes are provided by those arising out of situations of competition in which there are 'parallel efforts by both parties concerning the same prize'.[8] Such competition may focus on securing some position of leadership, or access to some scarce material resource valued by the disputants. In our own society struggles for political office and wage bargaining can be viewed in this way; the dispute being generated in the pursuit of an objective without any rule necessarily being broken. Disputes of this kind may be distinguished from those in which the quarrel directly concerns a broken rule; where, for example, one person has physically injured another or has behaved in relation to some material resource in a manner which is at variance with the accepted norms of the society concerned.

Although it may be valuable for some purposes to recognize a difference between disputes arising out of competitive activity and those associated with broken rules, we should be cautious about drawing any hard and fast distinction. As Comaroff has recently reminded us,[9] rules are not simply signposts indicating approved conduct, which may in practice be complied with or ignored, but also resources which may be used in the course of a dispute and ultimately invoked to rationalize the outcome. Thus the relationship between the source of a dispute and any rule which is broken may be a complex one. Disputants may break rules for strategic purposes in the course of some 'parallel efforts' towards the same goal. This provides one reason why there is no necessary correlation between the seriousness of the dispute and the importance of the rule broken. One party may, for example, break a trivial rule in the course of a quarrel arising out of a serious conflict of interest as a pretext for airing the more fundamental issue, perhaps enabling a relationship concerned to be tested, re-affirmed, changed or broken off. In the course of my fieldwork

8. Simmel, *Conflict*, p. 57.

9. 'Rules and Rulers: Political Processes in a Tswana chiefdom', *Man* (N.S.), vol. 13, pp. 1–20.

with the Kgatla in Botswana I repeatedly came across instances where the breach of some trivial rule appeared to be at the centre of some intractable dispute. I remember one case in which a woman deliberately broke her neighbour's cooking pot so as to obtain access to a forum in which a more fundamental grievance could be aired. In another case a man wrongfully detained someone else's billy goat overnight to provoke a complaint at the hearing of which a serious grievance as to their respective rights over some arable land and a well could be thrashed out. When the anticipated complaint was made, and the meeting to discuss it took place, talk was at first about the billy but very soon turned to the real issue over which the two men were at odds. The chance of discrepancy between the underlying causes of a dispute and the ostensible grounds on which it is fought must be present in any society; and the likelihood of this happening is only increased in a society like our own where the approved dispute-settlement agencies only entertain a dispute where it can be brought within the ambit of a recognized rule which has been broken.

B. THE HANDLING OF DISPUTES

We noted in Chapter 3 that societies differ widely as to the light in which trouble is viewed by the members and as to the amount of quarrelling which is seen as acceptable. In some societies peace and quiet is seen as essential and members cannot bear the least argument or disruption; in others there is constant shouting and noise, and people seem to relish a quarrel. Consistent with this, the reaction of individuals to trouble varies greatly from one society to another. On hearing that one of his cows had died, a Tswana tribesman in Southern Africa might allow himself a monosyllabic response, or even remain silent. Elsewhere such a reaction might be inconceivable, with a similar misfortune attracting what the Tswana man would see as an absurdly vivid display. Writing about Tangu in the New Guinea Highlands, Burridge noted that a grown male might respond to the news that one of his piglets had been accidentally killed (presumably an equivalent misfortune to the death of the Tswana man's cow) by 'whooping, yelling, leaping in the air, and thwacking his buttocks'.[10] Correspondingly, in the context of a quarrel, such differences of response may well be reflected in a disposition towards the conciliatory gesture on the one hand, and a readiness to reach for a spear on the other.

Whatever the origins of such widely different responses, whether (as seems most likely) these are exclusively cultural, or whether they have some foundation in biological make up, they tend at any rate to be closely related to the values and beliefs held in the societies concerned. In some, physical violence and aggression represent dominant values, whereas restraint and attempts to avoid controversy are equally representative of others. In the former case a swift and firm response to any wrong provides the approved reaction, while passive inaction is seen as a sign of weakness and inadequacy. While in some societies a man is expected to meet almost any form of wrong with immediate physical retaliation, and may rely on his close kinsmen to give him active support in this, elsewhere such a response would be strongly disapproved and a high value attached to achieving restraint, even under severe provocation.[11] In some communities the act of retaliation would place the actor on much the same footing as the original wrongdoer. A response representing the minimum which 'honour' demands in one society may thus seem an inconceivable over-reaction in another.

Given this link between the values prevailing in a society and the likely responses to trouble, we should expect to find considerable variation as to the way in which disputants themselves approach a quarrel. In one society unwelcome words or behaviour may be met with direct inter-personal violence; in another with attempts to harm or destroy through sorcery, witchcraft or invoking the wrathful intervention of some

10. 'Disputing in Tangu', *American Anthropologist*, vol. 29, no. 5, 763–80.
11. See Chapter 7.

divine being; while in a third moves towards conciliation and compromise may represent the most likely response.

Just as varied are the ways in which third parties may be expected to intervene. Here the conceivable range of possibilities must include: warnings to wrongdoers as to the consequences of future repetition; attempts to shame them through mimicry, ridicule or public exposure; withdrawal of existing forms of association and cooperation; diversionary activity to engage the thoughts and actions of disputants in another direction; some form of settlement-directed discussion; physical coercion; or attempts to channel the activity in a direction which enables the conflict to be dealt with in the ritual sphere. The possible objectives of third-party intervention may also vary. This might be directed towards: providing active support for one of the parties; destroying or removing a wrongdoer; 'paying him back' for what has been suffered; modifying future conduct (whether by persuasion or coercion) along acceptable lines; exacting compensation; securing a reduction of tension, or lowering of the 'temperature'; and the restoration of harmony, or of some other kind of balance.

Beyond all this we should also remember that those mechanisms which we recognized in Chapter 3 as helping to maintain order may also operate to bring a dispute to an end once it has arisen. For example, even where the threat of harm to relationships of reciprocal obligation may not prevent an individual from embarking on a disapproved course of conduct, the actual withdrawal of cooperation may ultimately force him to abandon it. Similarly, other mechanisms inherent in the way a society is organized may help to terminate a quarrel or at least reduce the level at which it is waged, irrespective of the reactions or objectives of individual disputants. Such a result may, for example, be achieved through the interplay of those conflicting ties of loyalty which are present in many social groups. The cohesive potential of such 'crosscutting ties' was observed early on by the American anthropologist Kroeber in his study of the Zuni Indians,[12] and has

12. *Zuni Kin and Clan.*

been confirmed in later reports from other societies. One of the best-documented examples is that provided by Colson in her work on the Plateau Tonga of Zambia.[13] Somewhat simplified, the relevant features of Tonga organization can be described as follows. Every Tonga belongs to one of the fourteen matrilineal clans of which this society is made up. These clans are exogamous and instead of being grouped together the members are dispersed throughout the numerous small villages of their territory. Despite their dispersal, subdivisions of them constitute support and vengeance groups ready to come to the aid of a member who is wronged or in trouble. However, within each village and to some extent over a wider geographical area around it, economic and ritual ties also bind groups of co-residents together. Thus, where a man of clan X who belongs to village A kills a man of clan Y who lives in village B, it is unlikely that two hostile groups will prove capable of isolation, as members of both lineages will be found within the respective villages. In practice, the configuration of cross-cutting ties is likely to be more complex than this, rendering it even less probable that discrete hostile factions will emerge and become locked in a serious quarrel. Beyond preventing wider conflict, Colson argues that these incompatible loyalties put pressure on the kin and co-residents of the disputants to seek a solution to the immediate quarrel. The plural groupings necessary to set up conflicting loyalties are not a feature of all acephalous societies, but wherever they are present we should consider their implications for the way in which conflict is handled.

In the chapters which follow we shall be examining further the mechanisms for handling conflict found in different societies. These inevitably exist in varied forms and combinations. As control mechanisms, some are capable of fine adjustment, while others are cruder and less flexible. At this point

13. 'Social Control and Vengeance in Plateau Tonga Society', *Africa*, vol. 23, 199–212; and *The Plateau Tonga of Northern Rhodesia: Social and Religious Studies*.

it is possible to map out only a rough typology of responses to trouble, providing a perspective against which the diverse institutions and activities described in later chapters can be viewed.

i. Inter-personal violence

In some societies direct inter-personal violence constitutes an approved mode of response, either by way of retaliation for violence already suffered or as a reaction to some other type of wrong. Where this is the case, some conventions typically exist regulating both the severity of the permitted aggression and the manner in which it is carried out. One widely reported form of restriction requires that the response must correspond to, and be no more severe than, the wrong that has been suffered: the notion of 'an eye for an eye, a tooth for a tooth'. In a number of societies the idea seems deeply entrenched that in response to a physical assault a like injury may be inflicted, but no more than that. In the case of the East African Gisu, for example, it is said that where a man is killed, his kinsmen must wait until the son of the killer is of the age of the man killed before the like retaliatory action is taken.[14] Radcliffe-Brown and other scholars have noted that retaliatory action is equally finely regulated in the case of some Australian aboriginal groups.[15] There, when a man is killed, his kin may retaliate against the wrongdoer or one of his kinsmen but the severity of the attack is strictly controlled. Spears are thrown and the victim is injured; but care is taken not to kill him, and the action stops when it looks as though fatal injuries are likely to be inflicted. Elsewhere detailed tariffs of acceptable retaliatory harm are found, listing the appropriate response to any form of physical injury.

As we noted earlier in the chapter, in some societies a wrong against an individual may draw in a range of his

14. Roscoe, 'Notes on the Bageshu' *Journal of the Royal Anthropological Society*, vol. 39, 181.

15. 'Primitive Law', *Encyclopaedia of the Social Sciences*, vol. 9, 202–6.

kinsmen to participate in redressive action, and a range of the wrongdoer's kin in support of him. Where this takes place, sporadic fighting may continue for sustained periods, and a feud develop which is capable of enduring long beyond the lifetimes of the original disputants. But even in these cases of inter-group conflict, conventions seem typically to impose limits on the level of violence resulting. Examples of this, drawn from the Sudanese Nuer and the Jale of New Guinea, are given below.[16] In both cases the level of violence which follows on an inter-group confrontation is restricted. Koch writes, for example, that in Jalemo the fighting is generally called off when one or two people have been killed. Similar limitations upon inter-group violence are widely reported.

One way in which a response involving direct physical violence seems very widely regulated is through its being channelled into a restricted and conventionalized form. The means through which this may be achieved can be seen from a few examples. Reay, writing about the Minj-Wahgi peoples of the Western Highlands of New Guinea, describes how disputes which come to involve two groups of kinsmen may be handled through an institution known as *tagba boz*. Two 'sides' from the opposing groups line up with their arms clasped behind their backs and kick at each other's shins until one group withdraws. A pig theft, or the stealing of some crops, may trigger off such an exercise.[17] Similar are the buffeting contests reported from several groups of Eskimo.[18] According to most accounts, two men involved in a dispute meet in front of an audience at a public gathering place and, standing opposite one another, deliver alternate straight-arm blows to each other's heads until one is knocked to the ground or gives in. A variation of this buffeting is provided by head-butting bouts in which the disputants sit opposite each other and butt with their heads until one is unseated by the impact.

16. See Chapter 7.
17. Reay, 'Changing Conventions of Dispute Settlement in the Minj Area', Epstein (ed.), *Contention and Dispute*, pp. 198–239.
18. See p. 93 below.

An essential feature of controlled conflict of this kind is that there are recognized conventions which delimit the struggle, and ideally have the effect of preventing death or serious injury on either side (although, as Reay notes in the Minj-Wahgi case, *tagba boz* can get out of hand and degenerate into a more serious conflict), thus making continuous and escalating violence unlikely. Another important aspect is that the conflict is to some degree removed from the issue in dispute (the stolen pig, the abducted woman) and directed into the 'game' which the contest represents. Accordingly, this method of handling a dispute has diversionary value. Further, these contests are presumably very exhausting, with the result that appetites for further fighting following them are usually diminished.

In societies with a centralized state organization the right to undertake redressive action is often taken altogether out of the hands of those who see themselves as being wronged. We see this happening in societies like our own, where in criminal matters designated officials ascertain responsibility and then administer punishment in accordance with carefully regulated scales.

ii. Channelling conflict into ritual

In examples such as the Eskimo buffetings and the Minj-Wahgi *tagba boz*, where the action is to some degree disso-ciated from the issue out of which the dispute arises and where the inter-personal violence becomes a highly formalized ex-change, the handling of conflict is already being taken over into the sphere of ritual. This process goes a stage further when the violence is excluded altogether and simply 'repre-sented' by some other form of activity. An example of this is the Eskimo *nith*-song contest. Under such a contest the 'two parties to a dispute or quarrel confront each other, before the assembled community, and voice their contentions through the medium of songs and dances improvised for the occasion'.[19] First, the accuser pours out all the abuse he can think of in the

19. Weyer, *The Eskimos*, p. 226.

form of a song; the accused then responds in the same terms. A whole series of such exchanges may follow until the contestants are exhausted, and a winner emerges through public acclaim for the greater poetic or vituperative skill. Bohannan, writing about the Tiv of North Eastern Nigeria, gives examples of song contests between two disputants and their followers which seem to fulfil a very similar function.[20]

In the same category are some of the competitive food exchanges which several scholars have reported from Melanesian societies. Here a famous example is provided by the Trobriand Islanders' *buritila' ulo*. This is a transaction involving the exchange of yams organized between two village communities where a quarrel has broken out. Malinowski gives a colourful account of one of these exchanges.[21] On the occasion he describes a quarrel arose between two men, who belonged to different villages, at the garden plot which one of them was cultivating. Insults were exchanged and both men questioned the quality of each other's yams. One then broke down the other's garden shed and a fight ensued. According to the socially accepted norms of the community concerned, kinsmen would have been expected to join in and support the men if nothing had been done to stop them. At first senior men from the disputants' respective villages took the part of their own kinsmen, and it looked as if warfare would thus break out. However, before it did so, a 'big man' of the group to which the owner of the garden shed belonged offered to present all the yams produced in his village to the members of the other. This challenge was taken up by the others, who agreed to present all their yams in return. Thereupon the members of the first village set to work furiously collecting, counting and measuring the yams from their various stores and making a wooden receptacle in which the tubers could be carried across to the adjoining community. This work took up their full attention, and they were exhausted by the time the yams had been carried across. When this operation was complete the

20. *Justice and Judgment among the Tiv*, pp. 142–4.
21. *Coral Gardens and Their Magic*, vol. 1. pp. 182–7.

members of the other village themselves began to collect and
check their own yams and prepare a container for their
transit. Again their energies were utterly absorbed in this task,
and by the time their yams had been carried across to the
other village they too were exhausted. The respective offerings
were judged exactly equal in size and quality by the members
of the two villages, so honours were seen to be even, and
there seems to have been no thought in anyone's mind of
pursuing the original quarrel over the yam-growing and the
garden shed. Malinowski suggests that if one village manages
(or chooses) to outdo the other in this presentation, rather
than the matter ending on a note of nice equality, fighting
between the two communities is likely to ensue. Thus it seems
a risky means of reducing conflict, although the chances of
those involved wishing to extend the quarrel too soon after
these exertions seem slight. The uncertainties inherent in this
type of exchange appear from other examples. Writing of the
nearby Goodenough Islanders' competitive food exchange,
the *abutu*, Young notes that it may do little to resolve the
dispute between the individual contestants, and provides no
guarantee that the outcome will be such as to leave the two
groups concerned on what they see as level terms.[22]

iii. Shaming

Rasmussen[23] reports instances in which Eskimo *nith*-songs are
used in a rather different way, as a form of public reprimand,
bringing home to someone guilty of anti-social conduct the
disapproval with which his behaviour is viewed. The singer
recounts the wrongdoing loudly in a public place where all
can hear, hoping to shame the wrongdoer into mending his
ways. Similar means of curbing disapproved conduct are very
widely reported, all of them involving some form of ridicule,
reproach or public exposure, operating to discomfort the
wrongdoer and thus encourage him back to acceptable forms
of behaviour. These include the 'public harangue' widely

22. *Fighting with Food*, pp. 207–27.
23. *Across Arctic America*, pp. 95–6.

reported from communities living in New Guinea and on the surrounding islands. In the course of one of these occasions a man's wrongdoings are embarrassingly exposed by being shouted out to the community at large. Speaking of the Kalauna community on Goodenough Island, Young says that harangues are 'preferably delivered from a house-step on a dark night' and 'since the village is compact enough for most of it to be within earshot of a single shouting voice, it is an efficient and satisfying way of bringing delicts to public notice. The message is assimilated in absolute silence, and if a particular individual is being accused, he will be found sitting inside his house with head bowed under the imagined stare of the whole community.'[24]

Attempts to curb anti-social behaviour through shaming need not take on a formalized character and are often found in the context of everyday conversation. Bloch notes that this was often the case with the Merina of Madagascar, and provides a neat example. Where thefts are discovered in a Merina community, one common way of dealing with them (whether the identity of the thief is known or not) is for people to sit round in the meeting place, speaking ruefully and pointedly of the evils of stealing in general, expressing their sadness at what has happened, and the hope that it will not happen again. Where this is continued over time it becomes too much for the wrongdoer to face and he desists from the disapproved behaviour.[25]

A silent but equally subtle form of reproach is used by the Orokaiva of New Guinea to deal with stealings.[26]

When a man finds his coconuts stolen he may tie a fragment of husk to a stick and set it up on a track near his palms; then everyone will see that a theft has been committed, and the thief, even though his identity remains unknown, will feel a pang of shame whenever he passes the spot. Similarly, the owner of a ravaged garden will affix a *taro* leaf to a coconut palm in the midst

24. *Fighting with Food*, p. 125.
25. M. Bloch, personal communication.
26. Williams, *Orokaiva Society*, p. 330.

of the village for all to see and for the special discomfort of the culprit.

From several societies there are reports of individuals attempting to reduce conflict in a similar way through the use of ridicule, poking fun at those guilty of anti-social conduct. Such people seem to fulfil a role similar to the one we associate with the medieval court jester, who, by virtue of his acknowledged position as a joker and buffoon, is able to convey serious messages in a light and humorous way. According to reports from some societies, cripples and others who are for some reason unable to take a normal part in the day-to-day activities of the community are often found in this role. Turnbull writes that, among the Mbuti, acknowledged clowns and buffoons take the edge off disputes by ridiculing and making fun of the disputants, diminish tension by their diversionary antics and pour scorn on any individual whose actions threaten the security and harmony of the group. Because of the jesting way in which these 'warnings' are conveyed, and because of their veiled character, such strategies avoid the possibility of retaliation which more abrupt and undisguised intervention might attract. The singing of rude and deflating songs to, or about, a troublesome individual is also reported as a means of achieving a similar end.[27]

iv. Supernatural agencies

The idea that supernatural beings may intervene to punish wrongdoing is very widespread. So too is the belief that harm may be inflicted by witches or through the practice of sorcery. Magical procedures are also used very widely to discover the source of harm which has been suffered, thus at least providing a staging-post towards its abatement. But the precise role which such ideas and practices play in the generation and handling of conflict must depend on the configuration of beliefs in a given society.

Although in most communities where sorcery is found its practice is feared and disapproved of, it may nonetheless be

27. *Wayward Servants*, pp. 182–3.

seen as a legitimate method of retaliating against a wrong which has been suffered. In some Melanesian societies, almost any form of wrongdoing is liable to evoke retaliation in the form of sorcery directed against the wrongdoer or his kinsmen.[28] Under such circumstances, the resort to sorcery corresponds to direct physical retaliation and may be viewed with even greater dread.

Witchcraft and sorcery are seen in some societies as a possible cause of death and of almost any form of illness or material misfortune. So where these incidents occur it becomes imperative to identify the witch or sorcerer concerned if existing harm is to be abated and further harm prevented. Identification will also remove the danger of quarrels associated with suspicion and accusation. Once the witch or sorcerer is found, retaliatory measures may be taken or efforts made to appease the anger which has led to the original attack. Thus, in many societies, the procedures for identifying witches or sorcerers responsible for a particular incident or misfortune assume great importance in the handling of conflict. We shall see in Chapter 6 the elaborate procedures which exist in Tiv society for identifying the witch who has caused some misfortune. There the history of events surrounding the death of Geza shows clearly how important this process of identification can be in restoring harmony in one West African society. Once the autopsy on Geza revealed the presence of *tsav*, earlier deaths were explained and the future made more secure. Geza was the witch responsible for these deaths; now he was dead himself he was beyond inflicting further harm, and peace could return among his kinsmen; a solution of great neatness from the angle of preventing further conflict, as the cause of earlier harm is at once explained and responsibility for it directed away from surviving members of the group.

The ordeal, familiar in our own history and found in many other cultures, may provide both the means through which a wrongdoer is identified and the instrument of his punishment. In the famous West African 'trial by sasswood', an accused

28. See Young, *Fighting with Food,* for the Kalauna example.

person is made to drink a preparation made up from the toxic bark of the sasswood tree. If he vomits up the poison he is innocent, and he will live; if the poison is ingested, he is guilty and will die. Warner has described another ordeal procedure which is followed among the Loma in Liberia.[29] There a person accused of theft or some other wrongdoing has to pluck a brass anklet from the bottom of a pot of simmering oil with only a paste of leaves to protect the hand from the heat. If the anklet is retrieved successfully without injury, the accused is innocent; if he is burned in the process he is guilty and has suffered his punishment.

v. Ostracism

Of the possible responses to trouble, withdrawal from association and cooperation stands at the opposite end of the spectrum to direct inter-personal violence. For quarrelling individuals or groups to part, either permanently or until the trouble is forgotten, is obviously one of the most effective means of handling conflict; but it is also potentially the most radical as it can involve serious disruption of the business of making a living. In many groups it represents the most dreaded sanction that can be threatened or imposed. It is also the one susceptible to the finest regulation and control, being capable of almost infinitely varied scale and severity. Whole groups may break up and disperse; individuals may be expelled from a group or temporarily withdraw; the parties to a dispute may remain physically together but modify or discontinue existing forms of cooperation; or wrongdoers may be ostracized in social and ritual matters, but nonetheless remain part of the support group.

The difficulty which ostracism presents as a mode of handling conflict lies in the fact that in the very act of putting the disputants apart, established processes in social life and the business of making a living are necessarily disrupted. At best this represents inconvenience, at worst it means starvation and death. At first sight, the separation of disputing groups or

29. Warner, *Trial by Sasswood*, pp. 50–51 and 241–7.

individuals represents the easiest solution to trouble in nomadic hunting and gathering communities. They are on the move anyway, so why not along separate roads? In some communities this is exactly what happens in practice, and many reports confirm frequent re-grouping on the move, often in response to friction.[30] But where the means of making a living is such that the cooperation of given numbers is essential, as is the case with certain forms of hunting, withdrawal from a group becomes a luxury that cannot be indulged unless alternative groups are readily available. Some reports from nomadic societies indicate that members live in constant fear lest trouble disrupt the group, leaving the component members unable to make a livelihood. In settled communities, separation potentially presents greater difficulties, given the investment in more permanent dwellings, laboriously cleared tracts of arable land and herds of stock. But even here it represents a solution to the more intractable forms of conflict that is quite widely followed. Indeed, in the case of some societies of shifting cultivators, the periodic break-up and re-grouping of village communities in the wake of struggles for political leadership seems to represent a normal and inevitable phase in the developmental cycle.

In any community less fundamental adjustments of association and cooperation must play an essential part in handling trouble and curbing anti-social behaviour. This was the point that Malinowski was making in his famous studies of life in the Trobriand Islands. There he showed how elaborate webs of reciprocal obligation operated to discourage quarrels and helped to bring them swiftly to an end where they did break out. Malinowski noted that the member of a Trobriand community who could not maintain the relatively peaceable relationships upon which the smooth operation of these essential economic operations depended soon found himself with no place in the community. He had the alternative of keeping in line or going to live 'as an unwelcome guest' in a far away community among distant kin. While ties of reciprocal

30. See pp. 84–5 below.

economic obligation are probably nowhere as exclusively effective as Malinowski saw them to be in the Trobriands, they play some part in regulating conflict in any community.

vi. Talking

Within any social group talking must be a principal means whereby trouble is avoided and through which efforts are made to resolve it when it does arise. Through talk people get to know what others are thinking and are going to do, as well as how their own actions are perceived, and are enabled to arrange their affairs accordingly. Where trouble does crop up, talking in the first instance provides a vehicle through which anger can be expressed and released, and then a means through which those involved can feel their way towards a settlement. It also provides an effective channel for third-party intervention in search of a settlement, whether in the informal atmosphere of the home, or the more formal setting of a law court.

It is sometimes suggested that trouble may be avoided in very small communities simply because, largely through talking, people remain in touch with what other people think and feel. As a group grows beyond a certain point, this intimacy in communication is lost and trouble becomes harder to avoid, just because people are out of touch. It has even been argued that this is a reason why certain nomadic groups seldom exceed a given size for long.[31]

Other scholars have emphasized the therapeutic effects of verbal exchanges once things have gone wrong and there is something to quarrel about.[32] Through talking and shouting you can 'get it off your chest', and the tension is accordingly lowered. But equally things can be made worse in the course of a verbal exchange. Words are uttered that would be better left unsaid, leading to more serious trouble and to fighting. In writing about his Trobriand research, Malinowski noted that some disputes got no further than shouted verbal exchanges

31. See p. 88 below.
32. See, for example, Gibbs, 'The Kpelle Moot: A Therapeutic Model for the Informal Settlement of Disputes', *Africa*, vol. 33, 1–11.

(*yakala*) in which two groups might confront each other in abuse and accusation. But while these 'native litigations', as Malinowski called them, could lower the temperature, they could equally operate to harden the grievance and end in fighting.[33] Other scholars have also argued that these shouting matches often raise the level of conflict. Koch, writing about a Jale community on the New Guinea mainland, noted that while 'exhaustion and tedium terminate an altercation' and 'participants become tired of repetitive speech and one by one drift back to the fireplaces of their men's houses', one of these exchanges may equally 'enhance hostility towards one's opponents'.[34]

At the same time, talking can offer disputants the possibility of reaching a mutually agreeable solution to their quarrel through settlement-directed discussion. In many societies such means are strongly approved, and should ideally be resorted to first, before appeals to third parties for help, as a preferred alternative to inter-personal violence. Yet in others, the possibility of bilateral discussion in the event of a dispute is hardly present. Honour may demand a more vigorous response, or else violent reaction is felt to be so near the surface that such bilateral contacts are liable to make the situation worse.

As I have already noted, talking also provides a basic channel for outside intervention. Often third parties intervene in a dispute explicitly to discuss the trouble; but they may also do so to steer the conversation away from it. We have all been involved in heated exchanges when some sensitive outsider has tactfully diverted the direction of discussion in some uncontroversial direction, and so aborted a quarrel. There are many references to such 'diversionary' modes of handling conflict in the anthropological literature. Instances are offered, for example, where the direction of discussion round the fire is skilfully led away from a delicate topic. Alternatively, a hunting expedition may be proposed with timely enthusiasm

33. *Crime and Custom in Savage Society*, p. 60.
34. *War and Peace in Jalemo*, p. 70.

when talk in camp looks like leading to a quarrel.

In the remaining section of this chapter we consider in more detail the different forms which settlement-directed talking may take. We begin by mapping out a rough typology, indicating the different postures which the disputants and third parties may take, and then consider those conditions favourable to each form and (in the case of those processes involving third parties) the attributes which intervening third parties are likely to require.

C. SETTLEMENT-DIRECTED TALKING

Many writers have noted different means of resolving disputes by talking about them and have attempted classification.[35] Some of their formulations have been incredibly detailed,[36] but for the present purposes we shall consider three basic forms which settlement-directed discourse may take: the disputants may feel their way towards a settlement through bilateral negotiation; they may try to resolve the matter with the help of a neutral mediator; or they may submit the quarrel to an umpire for decision.

Bilateral negotiation represents the least complex form of settlement process. Here the rival disputants approach each other without the intervention of third parties and try to bring the dispute to an end through bilateral discussion. No intermediaries or supporters are involved; the achievement of communication and the subsequent process of settlement lies in the hands of the two disputants alone. A variation of this mode of settlement is present where third parties align themselves in support of one or other of the disputants; but while the 'strength' of the respective sides may be altered by this

35. See, for example, Gulliver, *Social Control in an African Society*; Eckhoff, 'The mediator, the judge and the administrator in conflict-resolution', *Acta Sociologica*, vol. 10, 158; Gluckman, *Politics, Law and Ritual in Tribal Society*, pp. 183–96; Koch, *War and Peace in Jalemo*.

36. See, for example, Abel, 'The Comparative Study of Dispute Institutions in Society', *Law and Society Review*, vol. 8, 217–347.

procedure, the fundamental bilateral character of the encounter remains unchanged.

In each of the remaining modes of settlement this bilateral element is removed by the intervention of third parties in some intermediate position. Where this role is mediatory, the third party helps the disputants towards their own solution rather than imposing a solution upon them. The most limited form of mediation arises where the third party acts as a 'go-between'. His role is passive in the sense that while he operates as a bridge or a conduit pipe between the two disputants, he does no more than carry messages backwards and forwards between them. Through this means of communication the disputants themselves reach some kind of settlement. The go-between has not actively contributed to this settlement by giving his opinion, making value judgements, tendering advice or urging particular avenues of conduct; but he has enabled the disputants to communicate with each other. This form of mediation may be contrasted with a more active one in which the third party in a bridging position takes a positive part in promoting a settlement. His intervention may take the form of advice, suggested solutions, reasoned pleas, or even emotional cajoling, threats and bullying. Unlike the go-between, he actively pursues a settlement, while remaining ostensibly neutral and without seeking to impose an outcome.

Under the third mode of settlement the neutral third party seeks to resolve the dispute by making a decision, rather than assisting the disputants towards their own solution. Within this broad category it is important to distinguish two types of umpire, whom I shall label the arbitrator and the adjudicator. The arbitrator derives his authority to decide the dispute from the invitation of the disputants themselves, who have voluntarily submitted to his decision; while the adjudicator, who derives his authority from some office in the community, intervenes to impose a decision by virtue of that office rather than by the invitation of the disputants. In some respects this last distinction is of limited importance, as in both cases an authority to resolve a dispute in the face of competing claims by imposing a decision is present. Nonetheless, the distinct sources from which this authority is derived may, as we shall see later in this section, be of critical importance.

This typology underlines the crucial variables which attend these different processes: the achievement of a solution by negotiated agreement or imposed decision; the presence of third-party involvement; the nature of the intervener as partisan or neutral; and the derivation of authority in decision-making. But the processes identified will not always be crisply distinguished in practice. In the forms described they may appear distinct, but the various modes represent models only and in practice may shade off into one another. Even the broad distinction between bilateral negotiation and processes involving third-party intervention may break down where mediators emerge from the groups of supporters aligned behind each party. Similarly, where there is unanimity among the members of the respective support groups as to an appropriate settlement the disputants are in much the same position as they would be in the face of a decision by an adjudicator. They have no alternative but to comply with the proposed settlement, as failure to do so will imperil the future cooperation of their supporters. In many situations where third parties intervene in a bridging position between two disputants there may be lack of clarity as to whether the part played is of a mediatory or umpiring character. In one case X and Y may be disposed to accept Z's suggestions towards a settlement *because* he is renowned as someone even-handed and skilled in dealing with trouble; there Z's role as a mediator is unambiguous. On the other hand, X and Y may be disposed to accept Z's solution because Y owes Z cattle and X needs Z's help in some other enterprises; or Z may be a 'big man' upon whose patronage both X and Y rely. At some stage along the line the fact that Z proposes a given settlement becomes more important than the justification he advances in favour of that settlement. At a certain point still further, it becomes impracticable for X and Y to reject Z's solution; at that point Z looks like an adjudicator. Perhaps the best answer is to regard the mediator and the adjudicator as polar cases at different ends of a continuum along which these analytically distinct functions merge into one another in practice.

Against that background we can consider further the nature of these different processes, the conditions under which they are likely to be found, and the attributes of different kinds of intervener.

i. Bilateral negotiation

Negotiation takes place where disputants seek to resolve their quarrel without the help of neutral third parties. The minimal requirements are that the disputants should make contact on a level which makes talking possible, establish common ground for discussion and then feel their way by a process of give-and-take towards a negotiated settlement.

Superficially, these conditions look simple to achieve. All that is needed is for the parties themselves to want a settlement; there is no need to search for neutral third parties. But these basic prerequisites are in practice difficult to achieve, particularly where one party considers that he has been seriously wronged by the other. Under such circumstances it may be impossible for the parties to meet at all without the risk of escalating violence. Furthermore, any agreements reached may be hard to maintain without third parties to police them. Nonetheless, we shall see later that in some societies bilateral negotiation proves a perfectly satisfactory mode of settlement.[37]

ii. Mediation

We have defined the simplest form of mediation as provision of a conduit pipe through which messages can be carried backwards and forwards between disputants as they feel their way towards a settlement. Despite the limited nature of the go-between's role it is of immense importance in those cases where for some reason the disputants cannot meet together

37. See Chapter 7.

face-to-face. Such a situation may exist where tension is high and there is a risk of violence if they meet. Although it is clear from Evans-Pritchard's description that the Nuer 'leopardskin chief' performs a wider role than that of go-between,[38] that case illustrates the crucial role which the go-between can fulfil. Where, as in the Nuer example, the disputants cannot meet face-to-face because of the risk of retaliatory violence, negotiation is impossible unless a trusted neutral is available to convey messages between the disputants while some acceptable settlement is being hammered out.

Most mediators play a more active role than this in assisting disputants towards their own settlement. How they do this is succinctly described by Eckhoff: 'Mediation consists of influencing the parties to come to agreement by appealing to their own interests.'[39] In order to do this the mediator must first constitute a line of communication between the disputants, then help them to make explicit their respective positions and finally put forward the advantages of a settlement. The mediator may make use of several means in bringing this end about.

He may work on the parties' ideas of what serves them best ... in such a way that he gets them to consider their common interests as more essential than they did previously, or their competing interests as less essential. He may also look for possibilities of resolution which the parties themselves have not discovered and try to convince them that both will be well served with his suggestion.[40]

In doing so he may use threats, promises and flattery. So far as the nature of a mediated solution is concerned, this generally has the character of a compromise; but this ingredient is not necessarily inherent in the mode of settlement. The

38. *The Nuer*, pp. 163–75; see also below, p. 121
39. 'The mediator, the judge and the administrator in conflict-resolution', *Acta Sociologica*, vol. 10, 148, reprinted in Aubert (ed.), *Sociology of Law*, pp. 171–81. The page references here are to the latter version.
40. ibid., p. 171.

very fact that a proposed solution comes from a neutral third party may make it more acceptable to the disputants than it would have been had the suggestion come from one of themselves.

The conditions under which mediation is feasible and likely to succeed are implicit in the nature of the process itself. Eckhoff outlines them: [41]

> The conditions for mediation are best in cases where both parties are interested in having the conflict resolved. The stronger this common interest is, the greater reason they have for bringing the conflict before a third party, and the more motivated they will be for cooperating actively with him in finding a solution, and for adjusting their demands in such a way that a solution can be reached.

To a limited extent the mediator may help to create these conditions through his own activities but he may only do this where some disposition towards a settlement already exists.

The attributes of a successful mediator appear when he is contrasted with those who intervene in other ways in a dispute. In later chapters we shall see how people involved in disputes call upon close kinsmen and co-residents, upon co-lineage members and age-mates, upon specialists in religion and magic, and upon senior and influential people in the community, whether they are formal office-holders or not. Which class of person will be drawn into a dispute, and when, will depend on a whole range of variables; but of particular importance will be the capacity in which the help is sought. When a person is involved in a dispute he generally approaches third parties *either* because he wants to recruit their support and make them join his 'side', *or* because he believes that they will be able to help resolve the matter in an even-handed way – from a neutral standpoint – which will be acceptable to him and to the other party.

Different characteristics on the part of the person to be approached are called for in each case. In gathering a group of supporters a man will turn first to those who he feels will

41. ibid., p. 172.

be disposed to assist him or are under some obligation to do so. Such persons are most likely to be close kinsmen and those to whom he has himself given aid in some capacity in the past. The obligation to help a near kinsman in time of trouble seems widespread, and in some societies, like the Arusha and Nuer among those we shall consider, socially accepted rules indicate clearly which categories of a man's kinsmen will be expected to help in a dispute.[42] Similarly, some relationship of reciprocal obligation of another kind may form the basis on which assistance is sought. Where the disputant has lately helped one of his co-residents to clear a plot of land, or supported *him* in a dispute, he will expect this aid to be reciprocated. Gulliver's account of the Ndendeuli shows how relationships of economic cooperation may form the basis for demanding assistance in litigation.[43] While these considerations will probably define the field within which help is looked for, and the quality of support may to some extent be assessed in terms of numbers, an element of choice remains. A man will almost certainly turn first among those who owe him support to people with acknowledged skill in argument or whose influence and prestige in the community ensure that their views will be listened to.

In selecting a mediator, a disputant will look for a person who is not too closely identified with either side in terms of kinship or economic cooperation; someone who is, ostensibly at least, impartial. He will look, also, for an individual with special skill in this field, or who is for some other reason acknowledged as suitable for the role. Here the identity of the person concerned depends much on the nature of the society within which the dispute arises. If the community is made up of small undifferentiated groups of kin, age and proven skill in dispute settlement may be the paramount considerations. If the society is lineage-based, genealogical seniority may constitute an important consideration. Elsewhere some other criterion, such as particular piety, may

42. See p. 49 above pp. 128–34 below.
43. See pp. 123–8 below.

provide a recognized qualification for the mediator.

Mediators intervene in disputes where the disputants appeal to them or because they see themselves as having some independent interest in the outcome. Such interests may have to do with the security of the group as a whole, or with the personal prestige of the potential intervener. In small face-to-face communities, serious trouble between two members tends to threaten the security of the group, whether by forming harmful divisions within the group or by triggering off latent antagonisms among other members. At best a major quarrel which escalates will result in delays in essential jobs; and at worst, as we see in the Ndembu illustration, to the break-up of the community.[44] For this reason, third parties tend to intervene in an effort to reduce the level of a dispute whether they are invited to do so by the disputants themselves or not. Particularly if death, serious injury or major damage to property cannot be prevented, the dispute may quickly engulf the whole community. Evans-Pritchard's material on the Nuer, and Turner's on the Ndembu, illustrate this vividly. In most of the societies we shall consider, it would be inconceivable for an individual not to consult other members of his community in the event of trouble cropping up; even if he chose not to, the decision would hardly be respected where the dispute looked like setting the whole community at risk.

Third parties may also be prompted to mediate because their position in the community requires them to do so. We shall see how 'big men' and notables in some acephalous groups depend upon success in this area of activity for their continued prestige in the community. Frequently, as in the Ndendeuli case, an important source of influence lies in successful participation in dispute settlement, and consequently, any notable who feels he can bring a particular quarrel to an end will have a strong incentive to intervene.[45] Conversely, failure to mediate successfully may be disastrous for a 'big man's' standing. So the decision to intervene to

44. See pp. 112–13 below.
45. See pp. 123–8 below.

avert the conflict, or to temporarily absent himself from the community altogether, may be of critical importance in an individual's career.

iii. Umpires

The crucial difference between the mediator and the umpire is that the former assists the disputants towards their own solution whereas the latter reaches a decision for them. Some writers have also suggested that this distinction between mediating and decision-making necessarily implies major differences of technique. Eckhoff, for example, insists that the umpire must be more concerned with rules, while the mediator will be dealing with interests. As he puts it, the judge's 'activity is related to the level of norms rather than to the level of interests'.[46] He also suggests that the judge's work involves an assessment of what has happened already, whereas the mediator is more concerned with the future. While these further distinctions may be present in practice, it is suggested that they do not necessarily follow from the initial distinction which has been put forward. Appeals to socially approved rules are frequently crucial in mediatory activity. At the same time, while in many systems umpires do purport to follow norms strictly in decision-making, it is not a defining characteristic of their role that they do so. Decisions may be handed down on an *ad hoc* basis, in accordance with what seems best to the umpire in the individual case. We come back to this point again in Chapter 10, but it is also relevant when we consider the conditions under which umpires operate successfully.

At first sight, the conditions under which umpires can work are markedly different from those under which a mediator may operate successfully. While the mediator must reconcile the respective interests of the parties, the umpire, it may be argued, is released from this necessity in imposing a decision. If that is so, the arguments which the mediator can adduce in favour of a particular settlement will be decisive. Upon what

46. 'The mediator, the judge and the administrator in conflict-resolution', Aubert (ed.), *Sociology of Law*, p. 175.

the disputants see as the quality of these arguments (whether they touch the disputants' narrow interests, the future harmony of the community, or the integrity of some approved rule) will depend his success in bringing about a settlement. The umpire who resolves the matter by decision, by saying what is to be, is not so constrained in this respect; the quality of the arguments with which he justifies his decisions is immaterial. But this may nonetheless affect his overall legitimacy in his role. However, it is at that level that the distinction between arbitrators and adjudicators becomes important. Because the arbitrator depends for his authority to make a decision upon the disputants' agreement that he should do so, he must be sensitive towards their opinions as to what an acceptable decision might be; otherwise the chances of his decision being complied with, and of his being approached to deal with subsequent quarrels, will be small. Such considerations are not present in the case of the adjudicator who hears and decides a dispute by virtue of his office in the community. Not only is he *entitled* to hear the dispute but he is also likely to have force at his disposal to ensure compliance with his decision if the parties do not like it. Only in the much longer term can unpopular decisions affect his legitimacy.

The societies we shall be considering reveal wide differences as to the approved means of dealing with disputes, particularly in the extent to which direct inter-personal violence and the invocation of supernatural agencies are seen as acceptable. In some cases an insult or a physical injury, a wrongful taking or destruction of property, is likely to be met with immediate retaliatory action; perhaps in the form of a direct physical assault, perhaps through sorcery. In other cases this form of response is strongly disapproved, and the proper means of handling the matter is to negotiate some form of compensation, or to submit the quarrel to a third party for judgement or advice. The varied range of responses we shall come across raises difficult questions. Why, for example, do some peoples handle trouble by fighting or attempting to destroy each other by sorcery, whereas others generally undertake settlement-directed discussion? Again, how are we to explain the very varied forms which settlement-directed discussion takes, and the diverse ways in which third parties intervene in disputes? We return to these questions in Chapter 9 after the control institutions found in different kinds of society have been considered more closely.

5

Nomadic Hunters and Gatherers

We saw in the previous chapters that one society may differ quite markedly from another in the means through which order is secured and disputes are settled when they arise. In looking for reasons why this should be so one question which must be considered is how far the nature of the control mechanisms in a given group is linked to the manner in which the members make a living. Does a way of life which primarily involves hunting, gardening or herding *in itself* have implications for the way in which order is maintained? Here this question is examined in the light of the control institutions found in societies of nomadic hunters and gatherers; and in Chapter 6 we consider the implications of the more settled life which arable farmers follow.

The relatively few surviving societies of hunters and gatherers live in widely different surroundings and exploit quite varied resources; but some generalizations can be made about them. First, because they live off what they catch and collect in the wild, rather than off domestic animals and the proceeds of arable farming, they tend to be on the move for much of their lives, in search of the game or vegetable matter concerned. In some cases members of a group do not even return to given localities at particular seasons in the year. Repeated movement also requires that personal belongings must be confined to those few which can readily be carried from place to place. The nomadic life further prevents accumulation of large surpluses of food, which could not be transported even if the mode of living allowed them to be collected. The margins of life must therefore be narrow, not in the sense that the essentials of life will necessarily be scarce, but in the sense that efforts must continually be made to secure them. Due, similarly, to the way in which hunters and gatherers make a living, the groups they form tend to be small. Bands of fewer than a dozen have been reported from some societies, and the largest groups (found among the Eskimo and Australian aborigines) seldom exceed two or three hundred. Groups of twenty-five to fifty seem to be about average for most hunters and gatherers. Whatever the number of people in a group at a given moment, considerable fluctuations in size are common, whether on a seasonal or other basis.

Although we are not primarily concerned with form of social organization here, it is important to note some characteristics which are shared by most hunters and gatherers. First, bands are generally made up of small groups of undifferentiated kinsmen, and strong lineage or age-set organization seems rare. Secondly, societies of this kind typically lack any form of centralized government[1] and in some of them any move towards the exercise of leadership by an individual is strongly disapproved. In others transitory groups form round an influential individual, perhaps someone specially skilled in the kind of hunting or gathering practised by them; but this does not imply any notion of continuity of office, under which one leader succeeds another in accordance with socially accepted rules. Where a large band does gather round a particularly able hunter, it gradually dwindles away as he grows old or loses his skill; there is no question of one of his immediate kinsmen succeeding to his position unless he too possesses special skills or influence.

At this point we should also note one respect in which hunting and gathering societies seem to differ very much from one another. This relates to their beliefs about the nature of the universe, and hence concerns the extent to which supernatural agencies are seen to be important in the generation and handling of conflict. Rather little seems to be known about the

1. In this respect some of the North American Plains Indians are exceptional. See, for example, the Cheyenne with their chiefs, council and military societies: Llewellyn and Hoebel, *The Cheyenne Way.*

beliefs held in some of these groups, but what material is avail
able is suggestive of significant variation. In some cases super
natural beings are credited with responsibility for establish
ing man on earth, but with showing little interest in him
thereafter; whereas in other cases a continuing interest is evi
denced by a vigorous response to various forms of human con
duct. For example, the Siriono nomads, who inhabit an area of
tropical forest in North East Bolivia,[2] believe that a super
natural being placed men on earth, but played no further part
thereafter, interesting himself not at all in their day-to-day
activities. On the other hand, in the case of the Eskimo com
munities, spirit beings are taken to be closely interested in
human conduct and capable of inflicting harm on humans when
they notice actions which are displeasing to them.[3] We consider
the control implications of such differences later in the chapter

The shared characteristics of nomadic hunters and gatherers
limited as they are, have some general implications for the way
in which harmony is maintained and disputes are handled when
these arise. First the fact of frequent movement in itself goes
some way towards defining the area which socially accepted
rules need cover. We have already noted that there must, in any
society, be a body of mutually understood norms indicating
approved and disapproved forms of conduct and providing a
framework sufficient to enable members to predict each other's
actions in day-to-day matters. But in hunting and gathering
societies, these norms need not be very elaborate or wide
ranging. Where personal belongings are few and no surpluses
of food are maintained, hardly any rules about property are
required. Similarly, the absence of arable and grazing activities
diminishes the possibility of individuals or groups becoming
closely identified with particular tracts of land. Thus, the likely
area of disputes is confined to those having to do with mating
and access to consumer perishables. Disputes over personal
property and land (major sources of conflict in other societies

2. Holmberg, *Nomads of the Longbow*.
3. Weyer, *The Eskimos*.

are unlikely to arise. Therefore as a minimum the rules *need* only cover such matters as mating, the sharing of food resources and procedures followed in hunting and gathering operations (at least in so far as these require coordination and collective effort).

Notwithstanding the small groupings, minimal accumulations of property and lack of attachment to particular tracts of land found in these societies, the available reports suggest that the depth of detail in their normative systems varies very greatly from one society to another. Among the Hadza of Tanzania, for example, socially accepted norms seem close to the minimum; whereas in some groups of Eskimo the normative repertoire seems pedantically full and detailed. Writing about the regulation of Hadza mating, Woodburn states that the formation of marriage is attended by little ceremony and that marriage is established and signified by no more than the fact that the parties are together.[4] Correspondingly, a long period during which a man and woman remain apart may be interpreted by third parties as indicating an end of that relationship. Rules concerning the sharing of game are similarly sparse, beyond the fact that where larger game animals are killed by a member of a group anyone in the group at the time may share; and that certain parts of such animals, the *epeme* meat, are eaten by adult males alone. By contrast, many aspects of an Eskimo's everyday life are hedged about with detailed injunctions and prohibitions. These relate to the touching and using of certain objects, the performance of given kinds of work, and even the preparation and eating of different types of food. Among the Eskimo most of these rules are associated with belief in spirit beings; more is said later in this chapter about the importance of the supernatural in connection with social control.

The nomadic life of these hunting and gathering groups may in itself provide means of dealing with any dispute which

4. 'Ecology, nomadic movement and the composition of the local group among hunters and gatherers: an East African example and its implications', Ucko, Tringham and Dimbleby (eds.), *Man, Settlement and Urbanism*, pp. 193–206.

does develop. Woodburn notes that in the case of the Hadza quite minor tensions or dissatisfaction within a group may prompt a move, even where the food stocks in the area occupied have not been exhausted;[5] thus suggesting that a change of scene alone may be enough to deal with some types of quarrel through the 'holiday' effect which this achieves. Similarly, frequent movement, together with the fluctuations in group composition that are reported from some of these societies, indicates that people who find themselves in dispute readily resolve the matter by getting away from each other.

Dispersal is in fact the most widely reported means of dealing with trouble in communities of hunters and gatherers. Where a quarrel breaks out, the parties go their separate ways, keeping out of each other's sight, at least until their anger has died down, perhaps permanently. In some respects this solution is an obvious and easy one in a group where people are on the move anyway, where there is little property involved and no permanent attachment to a particular geographical area. But its feasibility will ultimately depend upon the environment in which the people live and the way in which they exploit it. If food is scarce or the system of hunting demands the cooperation of large numbers, the break-up of the group or the withdrawal of individuals may be impracticable. On the other hand, where food resources are plentiful and easily tapped, even solitary survival may present no problem.

Woodburn, in his studies of the Hadza, suggests that in the area of Tanzania where these people live there are sufficient quantities of fruit, vegetable materials and small animals to keep even a feeble or elderly person living on his own almost indefinitely. Though the Hadza typically live in groups of fifteen or so there are thus no strong pressures to remain in a group if tension develops. Because the terrain is hospitable enough to allow an individual to survive on his own, the break-up of a group does not threaten the lives of the members and dispersal is readily used as a method of resolving trouble when it arises. Even minor quarrels, or simply an ill-defined sense

5. ibid.

of dissatisfaction, may prompt the whole camp to break up and disperse.

Writing about the !Kung Bushmen of the Kalahari desert, Marshall paints an entirely different picture.[6] There she suggests that inhospitable country leaves the margins between survival and starvation narrow, making individual withdrawal or break-up a threat to the whole group (at least in the minds of the !Kung themselves). She describes the !Kung as living in constant fear lest disruptive conflict should develop, wrecking the survival capability of the whole band. Under such circumstances dispersal cannot represent the ready solution to conflict which it does among the Hadza; but conversely the fear of break-up helps to ensure that quarrels are patched up before they become disruptive. In the one case trouble is dealt with by dispersal; in the other, fear of dispersal's consequences holds the group together. However, Lee, who did work slightly later among a related group of Bushmen,[7] presented a situation corresponding much more closely to the one described by Woodburn for the Hadza. It may be that the discrepancy between the two studies partly reflects changing fashions in anthropology. Following early reports from Eskimo communities, who lived in undeniably harsh conditions, there was a tendency to see all nomadic hunters and gatherers as precariously scraping a living, and to stress the connection between cohesion and survival. Latterly, however, it has been shown that in some hunting and gathering societies conditions of 'primitive affluence' may be found, which place no pressure on the individual to remain in uncongenial company.

In the case of the Mbuti pygmies of the Ituri forests in the Congo, solitary survival is also seen to be impossible in the long term, and the threat of ostracism from the band represents an ultimate sanction against the troublesome individual. When one band banishes a member, others will refuse him member-

6. 'Sharing, Talking and Giving, Relief of Social Tension among the !Kung Bushmen', *Africa*, vol. 31, 231–49.
7. 'What Hunters Do for a Living', Lee and Devore (eds.), *Man the Hunter*, pp. 30–43.

ship, and alone in the forest he will die. But, short of this drastic measure, movement from one band to another represents a regular way of dealing with trouble. Mbuti bands disperse and re-group anyway on a seasonal basis, and Turnbull noted that, while the procedure was never explicitly discussed, individuals who had been quarrelling invariably ended up in different bands as a result of this re-shuffle.[8] Nonetheless, break-up at other times of the year was seen as precarious, particularly for members of a net-hunting band who relied closely on each other's cooperation; and the threat of disruption itself operated to sustain the continuity of the group. Holmberg similarly reports that in the case of the Siriono, while indefinite solitary survival was not possible, withdrawal for a limited period did sometimes provide a method of dealing with quarrels. He describes the case of a man who was burned when he rolled into the fire while wrestling at a drinking feast. The pain of his burns next morning left him furious with his adversary of the night before, and he left the camp for some weeks until his anger cooled.

These variations indicate that the literature's almost universal identification of dispersal as a means of resolving disputes in nomadic communities must be taken with caution. The feasibility of dispersal depends upon the environment and the way it is exploited. Thus polar cases can be identified: those where solitary life presents no difficulties and dispersal is therefore a ready solution to trouble; and those where an inhospitable terrain makes break-up hazardous (or it is at least believed to be so by the members of the society concerned), with the result that the feared consequences of disruption themselves operate to suppress conflict.

While fear of disruption may in itself operate to suppress quarrels another mechanism which is widely seen as helping to secure cohesion can be found in ties of reciprocal obligation. From almost all hunting and gathering societies some patterns of food sharing are reported, and from many of them cooperation in the catching or collection of certain types

8. *Wayward Servants*, pp. 100–108.

of food. Where such patterns of sharing and cooperation are formed between individuals, ensuing ties of obligation and reliance may provide very strong incentives for the partners concerned to avoid quarrelling. Marshall describes how all the members of a !Kung Bushmen band share in the larger game animals when one of the members catches one, and suggests that these repeated acts of sharing build up strong ties of mutual obligation and reliance. Reciprocal obligations of a slightly different kind arise among the Mbuti net hunters. Turnbull notes that while some Mbuti bands are composed of individuals who hunt alone with spears, others are made up of a group who hunt together with the use of a net. While net hunting does not involve much specialization or skill, a minimum number of people are needed to hold the net, and if too few are present or willing to cooperate the operation cannot be carried on. Thus, as members of net-hunting bands rely primarily on the proceeds of these hunts for their livelihood, individuals will hesitate to withhold cooperation in a hunt, or to withdraw from the band during those parts of the year when net hunting is practised. However, the force and generality of these reciprocal obligations must not be over-emphasized. As we have seen, the Hadza attach no very high value to group cohesion, yet Woodburn writes that all the members of a Hadza group are entitled to share the larger game animals when one of these is caught. Moreover, in this case the element of reciprocity is hardly a strong consideration as some Hadza males never succeed in catching one of the larger game animals throughout their lives, but are still permitted a share when others catch them.

Sharing can, equally, become a focus of dispute where one party feels that he is being treated less well than he has treated the other. Turnbull, while noting the cohesive value of relationships of mutual reliance among the Mbuti, particularly in the context of the net hunt, also observed that the time when a catch is divided may be an occasion of stress and suspicion.

The limited size of the groupings in which most hunters and gatherers live may also have an important influence upon the ways in which conflict is handled and prevented. In a small group each member is necessarily aware much of the time what others are saying (and to a lesser extent what they are thinking), with the result that the possibility of quarrels arising out of mis-understandings is diminished. Further, trouble can often be 'seen coming' by third parties, if not by the potential dis-putants themselves, and appropriate steps taken to deal with it. Among the !Kung Bushmen, Marshall observed profuse and free-ranging discussion among the members of a band and found this to be very important in preventing and reducing conflict. She also noted that where there was tension between two individuals and they failed to discuss the problem, other members of the group would deliberately do so within their hearing to ensure that the matter got fully aired before it blossomed out into a disruptive quarrel. Woodburn, noting that larger Hadza groups were more prone to fragment than smaller ones, considered one reason for this to be that the reduced intimacy of the larger groups meant less mutual under-standing and hence an increased possibility of dispute. Not-withstanding these observations, talking can have an opposite effect, and vigorous and frank discussion can exacerbate a problem. Marshall, among others, mentions the elaborate efforts which sometimes have to be made to steer camp-fire conversations away from potentially explosive themes.

One control mechanism which might be expected to assume particular importance in small face-to-face communities is that of shaming. Predictably, many accounts of nomadic hunting and gathering communities, notably those in which the pre-carious nature of everyday life is stressed, emphasize the effectiveness of shaming and ridicule as a means of handling conflict. Where survival is seen in terms of group membership, the threat of loneliness is unbearable and any sign of disap-proval or rejection deeply feared. We have already noted Mar-shall's observations concerning the discomfort which even mild disapproval generates in a !Kung Bushman.[9] Under such cir-cumstances she reports that the singing of rude and deflation-

9. See p. 40 above.

ary songs is typically effective in bringing the most hardy and troublesome individual back into line.

In the case of the Mbuti shaming and ridicule are carried out through the use of mime. The conduct of anyone who misbehaves is mimicked in public in an absurd and exaggerated way which brings disapproval home to the wrongdoer and leaves other members of the community in no doubt as to whom the display is aimed at. Among the Mbuti mime is one of the few forms of specialization encouraged, and some people develop into acknowledged clowns and buffoons who habitually take the edge off disputes by miming the disputants and pouring scorn on any individual whose conduct threatens the harmony and security of the group. Because of the jesting way in which these 'warnings' are conveyed, the possibility of retaliation (which more abrupt and undisguised intervention might attract) is avoided. The advantage of such a mechanism is that the acknowledged clown can use his mimicry even against a skilled and powerful hunter who might not tolerate criticism from another quarter.

The Eskimo *nith*-songs, as well as being used as weapons by disputing individuals,[10] also provide a medium through which a member of the community who is guilty of anti-social conduct can be publicly shamed. Rasmussen relates how an Eskimo called Kanaijuaq quarrelled with his wife and then tried to leave her and their child to perish in the wilds.[11] Fortunately the woman managed to get back to other people on her own, but Utahania, a friend of Kanaijuaq's reproved him before the assembled neighbours through this song,

> Something was whispered
> Of Man and Wife
> Who could not agree.
> And what was it all about?
> A wife who in rightful anger
> Tore her husband's furs across
> Took their canoe
> And rowed away with their son.

10. See pp. 59–60 below.   11. *Across Arctic America*, pp. 95–6.

> Ay-all who listen,
> What do you think of him,
> Poor sort of man?
> Is he to be envied,
> Who is great in his anger
> But faint in strength
> Blubbering helplessly,
> Properly chastised?
> Though it was he who foolishly proud
> Started the quarrel with stupid words.

Kanaijuaq retorted with a song about Utahania's own mis-behaviour at home, but the message was conveyed. These occasions enable warnings to be put across and grievances aired under circumstances which make it unlikely that the trouble will be further inflamed.

Where quarrels do arise within the small close-knit communities of which many of these societies are made up, they have to be dealt with swiftly and decisively if they are not to disrupt the essential business of making a living. At first sight direct physical retaliation against a wrongdoer or one of his kinsmen represents a speedy and effective mode of redress; but in a majority of nomadic hunting and gathering communities its exercise is subject to severe restrictions, making it at most a tolerated rather than approved response. Within many of these societies, there seems to be recognition that direct action is apt to intensify any dispute, and rather than contributing to its resolution serves to disrupt essential activities.

In some groups nothing is more greatly feared than the outbreak of inter-personal violence, which is seen to lead surely to the fatal disruption of essential food-gathering tasks. This is the case with the !Kung, who dread the outbreak of violence within the community. 'Occasions when tempers have got out of control are remembered with awe. The deadly poisoned arrows [with which !Kung hunt their game] are always at hand. Men have killed each other with them in quarrels – though rarely – and the !Kung fear fighting with a conscious and active fear. They speak about it often. Any expression of discord ("bad words") makes them uneasy.'[12] For them, fighting within the group spells its disruption and the likelihood of starvation for all the members. Consequently, trouble must be handled through other means than violence. According to Marshall, this is largely achieved in the !Kung case by suppressing open conflict altogether.

The Eskimos represent one of the very few groups within which scarcely regulated violence seems commonplace, even within a small community of co-residents. In their case killings repeatedly occur, particularly in connection with disputes over women. Rasmussen[13] notes that in one group of fifteen families that he visited there was not a single fully-grown male who had not been involved in some way with a killing. He related several cases, of which the following is a stark example. A Padlermiut man, Igjugarjuk, was repeatedly rebuffed by the family of a girl he wanted to marry. Eventually, he hid outside this family's hut and shot them all down as they came out, sparing only the girl concerned. She became his wife.

Killing also seems to be the socially approved means of dealing with the recidivist whose acts persistently endanger the peace of a community. Freuchen[14] tells the story of a young Greenlander who was ultimately killed by his own mother after a career of misdemeanours, including repeated lying – a very serious form of wrongdoing in Eskimo communities. The succession of wrongs began when the boy falsely reported the arrival of a visiting ship on the coast where he was living and then pelted those who came to see it with rotten eggs which he had collected. Thereafter he took other hunters' gear without permission, left open food caches when he borrowed from them and finally tricked the wife of a neighbour into sleeping with him, convincing her that he had the permission of her husband. At her wits' end, the boy's mother strangled him with a seal-skin rope as he lay asleep one night. Freuchen

12. 'Sharing, Talking and Giving, Relief of Social Tension among the !Kung Bushmen', pp. 231–2.
13. *Across Arctic America*, p. 250.
14. *Arctic Adventure*, pp. 123–4

reports that this deed was greeted with general approval in the community.

In a case like that of the young Greenlander, retaliation by kinsmen of the deceased is unlikely, and direct action of this kind does not have an unstabilizing effect on the community where it takes place. But in many groups such action seems to be regarded as the source of more difficulties than it resolves, and retaliatory violence is therefore hedged about with considerable restrictions. In the case of some groups of Australian aborigines, the escalating effect which direct action may have is the explanation which they themselves offer for the forms of limited and controlled retaliation which they practise. In some of these groups a man may be taken and speared by the kinsmen of the individual he has killed; but in carrying out this retaliatory action care is taken to throw the spears in such a way that vital organs are not pierced and the exercise is called off before fatal injuries are inflicted.[15]

In almost all of these communities there seem to be socially approved rules as to the form which retaliatory action may take and the circumstances under which it may be inflicted. Turnbull notes that 'The rules of self-help among the Mbuti are quite simple. It is perfectly proper to hit someone with anything wooden; it is not at all proper to draw blood, nor to hit anyone on the forehead, which is considered a dangerous spot. In the frequent marital disputes, any man who hits his wife on the head or in the face promptly loses any sympathy he might have had from his fellows.'[16] In the Mbuti case, the rites associated with the *molimo* festival also provide an occasion for controlled retaliatory violence. On the occasion of this festival the young men of a community go on the rampage through the village tearing leaves from the thatch of people' huts. Turnbull observed that while a token leaf was plucked in most cases, the huts of people who had lately been behaving in an anti-social way suffered much more serious damage.[17]

15. See p. 57 above.
16. *Wayward Servants*, pp. 188–9.
17. *Wayward Servants*, p. 114.

Holmberg's account of the wrestling bouts associated with Siriono drinking feasts suggests these examples of regulated violence may operate to reduce tension in a similar way. On these occasions the drinking is accompanied by and interspersed with wrestling among the men, which provides opportunities for getting rid of pent-up grievances and hostility. In the climate of intoxication which prevails serious harm is rarely inflicted, and everything seems to be forgotten by the time the contestants ultimately wake up next day.[18]

Apart from killings, the resolution of disputes through formalized and controlled combat is also reported from Eskimo groups. According to most accounts, the disputants meet in front of an audience at a public gathering and, standing opposite one another, deliver alternate straight-arm blows to each other's heads until one is knocked to the ground or gives in. This is seen to conclude the matter, in much the same way as the outcome of a contest between two medieval knights over a lady. Important here is the fact that the conventions of the contest are fixed so as to ensure a conclusion without death or serious injury resulting on either side; so continuing, escalating violence is made unlikely.

Another attribute of these buffeting contests is their diversionary value, as they enable the energy of the disputants to be exhausted in a manner which distracts them from the original issue in dispute. The same is true for the kinsmen of the disputants and other observers of the contest. Their attention and interest is drawn away from the original dispute and achieves a new focus in the entertaining spectacle of regulated combat. A variation of these contests is provided by head-butting bouts in which the disputants sit opposite each other and butt with their heads until one or the other is unseated by the impact. This diversionary element, under which potentially disruptive violence is dissipated in directions where it will prove harmless, is present in many forms of regulated aggression. In the Mbuti case we saw, for example, how violence was channelled off into ritual at the *molimo* festival. There it is clear that the

18. *Nomads of the Longbow*, pp. 156–7.

diversionary value of these rites is recognized by the Mbuti themselves. For Turnbull noted that the *molimo* was a festival which could be proclaimed at any season and that often when quarrels threatened to become disruptive its commencement would be hastily announced, directing the thoughts and activities of the group into observances during which parochial worries and grievances would be forgotten.[19] The Eskimo *nith-songs*, which have already been mentioned,[20] fulfil a similiar role, under which the energy generated in a dispute is channelled off in a harmless and entertaining way. There the quarrel is expressed in, and fought out through, a song; and an outcome is signalled in the relative acclaim which the two contestants enjoy.

One respect in which societies of hunters and gatherers differ a great deal from each other is in the extent to which fear of supernatural agencies is seen to be important in the prevention and handling of conflict. In cases like that of the Siriono[21] belief in supernatural agencies has minimal importance in this sphere. For the Mbuti, on the other hand, the forest is seen as an interested and largely benevolent divinity, which may nonetheless express displeasure at everyday events. 'An excessive storm, falling trees, poor hunting and ill-health' can all be taken as signs of displeasure. What the forest dislikes is quarrelling, 'noise'; so any of these occurrences may be taken as a signal of the forest's displeasure and as an indication that any current quarrel must be patched up. But even in the Mbuti case belief in supernatural agencies does not hold the central importance from the point of view of control which it does among the Eskimo. From nearly all the published data on these groups, it appears that fear of supernatural action is always present in everyday life and has a significant influence on conduct, with steps constantly having to be taken to avoid supernatural intervention, or mitigate its consequences when it has

19. *Wayward Servants*, p. 259–67.
20. See p. 59 above.
21. See p. 82 above.

taken place. Their system of beliefs can be summarized in the following terms: there are spirit beings who have power to harm man; some acts of men are displeasing to them, and where such acts are performed the spirit being can withhold desired objects or inflict harm, particularly ill-health, on the person or community concerned. Because all in the community may be harmed by some displeasing act, all have an interest in seeing that spirit beings remain satisfied and pose no threat to the overall security of the group.[22] Among these beings, those of constant importance in daily life are the souls of animals killed for food and other purposes. Provided the rules associated with each type of animal are complied with, the soul remains benign, but if they are neglected then the soul becomes angry and causes the wrongdoer and other members of the community to fall ill. Here a fundamental principle is that the respective products of land and sea are inimical to one another and must be kept apart at all costs. Thus, caribou and walrus meat, for example, must be eaten at different times, stored separately, and clothing and equipment used in pursuit of each must be kept apart and never interchanged. Alongside this principle there are numerous other regulations. For example, caribou are particularly susceptible to 'contamination' by women, so they must be skinned in such a way that women do not touch certain parts of them; and in pregnancy and at some stages in the menstrual cycle a woman must not eat or even touch caribou at all. Ill-health is seen to follow from the neglect of any of these regulations, so constant care has to be taken in ordering the simplest procedures in everyday life. Where one of these rules is broken, the only means of avoiding harm is through prompt confession to other members of the community. Occasional breaches of these regulations seem readily forgiven in Eskimo communities, but persistent offenders are reported to be banished or killed.

In the context of these beliefs the Eskimo religious specialist, the *angakok*, with his assumed access to and understanding of the spirit beings, can play an important part in handling

22. See Hoebel, *The Law of Primitive Man*, pp. 69–70.

conflict. Particularly where an epidemic breaks out, quarrels develop as people speculate as to who the culprit may be. Under such circumstances, the *angakok* may contain the trouble by using his powers to confirm that the ill-health is attributable to something displeasing to a spirit being and to identify the culprit. Once he has done this he coaxes the necessary confession out of the wrongdoer concerned at a public gathering and then prescribes a remedy. Being assumed to enjoy these powers, the successful *angakok* can exercise considerable secular influence in the community and manipulate its members through the remedies he suggests to appease the anger of the spirits. Instances are reported of these *angakoks* collecting revenue, ordering husbands and wives to separate, and making women have sexual intercourse with designated males as acts of atonement for some guilty conduct identified as the source of the misfortune concerned. In a society of this kind the relationship between access to the supernatural and secular power is obviously close and complex.

The use of sorcery in handling disputes is also widely reported in Australian aboriginal communities. In the case of the Gidjingali, for example, any person is believed capable of inflicting pain, illness or even death on an enemy.[23] Consequently, when sickness strikes people turn in accusation to those with whom they have had a quarrel. Either the quarrel can be patched up, and the other party persuaded to reverse the magical procedure which has brought on ill-health, or counter-measures can be taken to inflict harm upon him through sorcery.

Although the intervention of third parties as peace-makers seems almost universal in disputes between two members of a community, even when the trouble does not immediately threaten the security of the group as a whole, the mode of intervention varies greatly. Reports from many nomadic hunting and gathering communities suggest that in their case such in-

23. Hiatt, *Kinship and Conflict: A Study of an Aboriginal Community in Northern Arnhem Land*, p. 119.

tervention seldom takes the form of attempts to arbitrate in a dispute or to reconcile the parties concerned. Rather, these efforts seem more often directed towards some indirect means of reducing the conflict, such as pointing out in abstract terms the harm which will come to the community if trouble persists, creating some form of diversion, or laying the blame elsewhere. One reason for the prevalence of such indirect means is that in many hunting and gathering societies any movement towards acquisition of individual authority is strongly disapproved. There is therefore no-one with authority to arbitrate or even to intervene as an active mediator. The Mbuti settlement processes which Turnbull describes seem typical in this respect. There, any attempt to assume individual authority is swiftly met with scorn and hostility, with the result that no-one in a band is in a position to adopt an umpiring posture. Nor do third parties try to bring the disputants together by direct mediation. Instead intervention typically takes the form of diversionary activity, pouring scorn on the disputants, or the intervener holding himself to blame. We have already noted how third parties may suggest hunting expeditions or proclaim the beginning of the *molimo* festival in moments of tension. Turnbull also describes repeated incidents in which third parties took the heat out of disputes by attempting to assume blame for the trouble themselves.

A set of values inimical to the emergence of individuals capable of intervening directly in disputes is not necessarily found in all hunting and gathering societies, and in some leaders are openly recognized. In certain societies, for example, bands regularly form round particularly skilled hunters, with the members relying heavily on their prowess. Where such a situation exists those in dispute are likely to pay heed to the leader's opinions and be loath to disregard his views as to an appropriate settlement.

The clearest descriptions of third parties acting in mediatory and adjudicatory roles in a society of hunters relate to the Cheyenne Indians. One of the recognized duties of a Cheyenne Chief was that 'he should be a peace-maker – should act as a mediator between any in the camp who quarrelled'.[24] It also was the responsibility of the Council of Chiefs to impose punishment in cases of serious wrongdoing, such as banishment for murder; and the Cheyenne military societies are reported to have imposed decisions in disputes in which their members became involved.[25]

The relative importance of different control mechanisms in a hunting and gathering society thus depends as much upon the nature of the environment and the means of exploiting it as upon the political organization, values and beliefs of the community concerned. Where the climate and terrain are so harsh that the margins between survival and death are narrow, or where the means of making a living is one which requires close cooperation, mechanisms which secure cohesion of the group will acquire great importance. Where, on the other hand, subsistence is easier to achieve and not necessarily dependent upon cooperative effort, other mechanisms – notably dispersal – may be prominent. While it would be wrong to say that it was once universally assumed that the lives of all hunters and gatherers were spent under conditions of bitter hardship, most older studies certainly depict a hazardous life in which the margins between survival and starvation are small, and under which everything depends on the cohesion and cooperation of a group. Where this represents a true picture it is easy to see the value that must be attached to relationships of mutual reliance, and the lengths to which people will go to avoid a potentially divisive quarrel. However, a majority of more recent reports conveys a rather different picture which suggests that, in some hunting and gathering societies at least, the life is one of relative ease and security, under which small groups (and even persons living alone) can provide themselves with sufficient food for survival without working for it very hard. Under such circumstances of 'primitive affluence' the importance of group cohesion must be reduced, and the incentive to stay on in a

24. Grinnell, *The Cheyenne Indians*, vol. 1, p. 336.
25. Llewellyn and Hoebel, *The Cheyenne Way*.

group if one does not get on well with the other members will disappear.

In these societies, as in any others, disputes are going to flare up from time to time, and have to be dealt with when this happens. How this is achieved again depends to a significant extent upon constraints imposed by the environment. Thus, where frequent movement from one group to another and the attendant fluctuations in group size are both logistically feasible and seen as acceptable, dispersal provides a ready means of keeping quarrelling individuals apart. But where group cohesion is (or is seen to be) essential to survival this means of handling trouble is ruled out. To some extent also, those mechanisms which operate to prevent a dispute arising in the first place may help to bring it to an end if it should arise. Thus, while the fear of valued cooperation being withdrawn may be ineffective to prevent trouble coming into the open at all, its actual withdrawal may be successful in bringing the matter to an end. So, a lazy or quarrelsome member of a group may be forced back into line after suffering a period during which the support of others is withheld, even though earlier threats of withdrawal may have been unsuccessful. Whatever the means of handling conflict which are resorted to, open quarrels cannot be allowed to continue long in a small face-to-face community where survival depends on regular expeditions in search of food. One response can be to suppress quarrels so far as possible, as the !Kung Bushmen seem to. If quarrels are not suppressed in this way, they must be dealt with swiftly and decisively before they disrupt the business of making a living.

6

Settlement and Property

The change from hunting and gathering to a way of life which relies upon cultivating the soil necessarily has implications for the manner in which order and continuity are maintained. The need for some ground rules about sexual access and the sharing of food remains; but to these arable farmers require others to be added, bringing with them further control mechanisms, the substance of different kinds of quarrel and the means to deal with these as they arise.

The practice of agriculture demands fixed residence in a given geographical area for at least part of the year. This period must generally be such as to allow land to be cleared and cultivated, the crop to be sown, protected while it grows and finally harvested. These activities are thus carried out in the company of a more or less stable and continuing group of co-residents; a sharp contrast to the nomadic group with its fluctuations in size and composition. Further, with settled residence goes at least the possibility of much larger groupings than are found among hunters and gatherers, as arable farming generally allows a greater population density.

At the same time, settlement may demand different and more elaborate forms of cooperation to those necessary in hunting and gathering. These will centre on the building of permanent dwellings and on the farming operation itself. Careful coordination may be required if everyone's field is to be prepared and planted in time for a short growing season. Cooperation may also be demanded for defensive purposes as it is harder for a farming community to melt into the trees in the face of a potential enemy than it is for a band of hunters and gatherers.

Two other developments coming with a more settled life are

the possibility of accumulating property and the development of a different relationship with the land. Such property will take the form of more durable dwellings, farming implements and household goods, as well as any surpluses which may be incidental to the farming operation. Property may also lie in enduring rights over specific areas of arable land. In those societies which practise shifting agriculture, moving on every few years as a newly cleared area becomes exhausted, people are unlikely to establish a permanent relationship with a particular tract of land; but where settled agriculture is practised, durable rights may come to be recognized as residing in particular individuals or groups.

Lastly, agriculture may bring more leisure. While the business of keeping alive typically involves work for at least part of every day in a hunting and gathering band, farmers may be able to live off each season's crop, with little that has to be done in the interval between one harvest and sowing again for the next.

All these concomitants of agricultural activity have important consequences for the way in which order is maintained and disputes are settled in a given society. The first of these lies in the increased number of rules which these varied activities necessitate. As we saw, in a community of hunters and gatherers, a very limited normative repertoire can provide an adequate basis for social life. Both with the formation of close and enduring relationships with particular tracts of land, and with increasing possibilities of accumulating other forms of property, a much more complex rule-base becomes essential. It must allow for such matters as access to residential and arable land; the control and consumption of crops; the management and enjoyment of surpluses; and the devolution of rights over land and movables from one generation to another. The point may be simply illustrated through the cases of control over access to land and of property devolution. While the right of one person to hunt over a given area of land may necessitate only minimal restrictions upon the right of others to do the same, successful arable farming involves excluding others from the plot concerned, at least for part of the year. Such a restriction implies rules about distribution of land (governing the manner in which the right to cultivate a given spot may be acquired) and rules limiting the access for other purposes of remaining members of the society to a level compatible with successful farming. Obviously rules of these kinds assume greatest importance where settled agriculture is practised and where good arable land is scarce, but they must be present in some form wherever land is tilled. Similarly, rules concerning the devolution of property in a society of hunters and gatherers will be vestigial if they exist at all, as there is so little in the way of property to pass from one generation to another; but the animals, farming implements, household goods and more durable dwellings associated with settled life may be highly valued property requiring explicit rules about inheritance. The same will be the case with arable lands, except in those cases where shifting agriculture is practised and the soil is so poor that plots are typically abandoned after a season or so's use.

In the context of this broader rule-base a new range of potential disputes is opened up. These include quarrels over the best situated residential sites and the most favourable arable tracts; over the produce that becomes available as a result of successful arable activity; over the help which kin or co residents expect of each other in connection with clearing cultivating and reaping activities; and over the devolution of interests in land and movables when someone dies. Thus to disputes over perishable food and sexual access already noted in hunting and gathering societies is added a class of disputes over the management and enjoyment of valuable durable property.

The nature and frequency of quarrels may also be related to the periods of leisure which successful arable farming provides for at least some members of a society. Where such leisure is found, opportunities for gossip and quarrelling are enhanced with fighting and the exchange of abuse more likely to flare up. It is not surprising that under these circumstances reports from several societies suggest that the incidence of disputes arising out of fights, injuries and the use of bad language fluctuates on a seasonal basis with most bunched in those periods of maximum leisure. In some societies the likelihood of such disputes is also heightened by the increase in brewing activity which often attends successful arable farming. While the preparation of alcoholic liquor from honey and other substances is sometimes found in hunting and gathering societies, the scale and ease of such operations is greatly enhanced by the availability of cereals and root crops. In some societies inter-personal violence and serious exchanges of abuse are predominantly associated with beer drinking.

Some of the implications of group size were considered in the previous chapter. As we saw there, the possibility of disputes arising may be reduced in a small group where all the members are in close touch with each other and have the opportunity of knowing what is being thought and said. In the larger groups that may be found in a farming village this will not be so, with the possibility that harmful conflict may arise out of misunderstanding as groups and individuals get out of touch with each other. Against that, a larger community may allow people in dispute to distance themselves from each other while anger cools or peace-makers try to sort things out.

Compliance with a broader rule-base, regulating as it does more complex and wider-ranging activities, still has to be secured in many societies of arable farmers without centralized governmental organization and agencies directly capable of seeing to enforcement. Because of this, most of the mechanisms which we considered in the previous chapter retain primary importance. Among these, ties of reciprocal obligation, the use of shaming and ridicule, and the work of supernatural agencies acquire new emphases in the context of farming activities.

Where members of a society depend for a living on arable farming, the tasks of clearing, planting and reaping may well form a primary source of reciprocal obligations if these operations are beyond the capabilities of an individual household acting on its own and thus demand the cooperation of other groups. Often this cooperation will require sophisticated planning if the land of all members of a community is to be cleared and prepared in time for the growing season. Gulliver describes this process vividly in his account of the Ndendeuli of Southern Tanzania which we shall consider further in Chapter 7.[1] The Ndendeuli live in woodland areas where poor soil necessitates a move to fresh fields every two or three seasons, and following such a move each household requires the help of other members of the community if new fields are to be cleared, hoed and planted. For this purpose the head of each household forms a clearing party to help with the work, and himself joins the parties of those people who help him. In any society where, as in an Ndendeuli community, major and essential tasks in the arable cycle require the cooperation of members and other households, a man will be careful to avoid acting in such a way that people will be unwilling to extend to him the necessary cooperation.

The formation of these ties may well extend beyond the primary tasks of raising the crops, as we have already seen by the examples from the Trobriand Islands which Malinowski provides. There we saw the relationship which developed between the inland cultivator, depending for his fish supplies on a littoral partner, whom he in turn supplied with yams.[2] But in the Trobriand case further complexity lies in the fact that the yams which the cultivator provided for the fisherman were not grown by himself, but by his wife's brother. For, in the Trobriands, as was explained previously, instead of each man growing for himself the yams necessary to feed his household (and maintain his exchanges with his fisherman), his efforts are directed towards providing for his sister and her husband, while his own needs in this respect are met through the labour of his wife's brother. It is easy to see how the breakdown of any one of these relationships in which an individual is involved may have disastrous implications for the remainder; and there will

1. See pp. 123–8.
2. See pp. 38–9.

thus be a strong disincentive to indulge in any form of disapproved conduct which might threaten a source of supply.

This Trobriand example is of further interest in that it draws attention both to the potential uses of *surplus* produce, and to the links which may develop between farming activities and marriage. The surpluses of arable farming, difficult to store over long periods, can sometimes be invested profitably in strengthening social relationships. Anthropological studies have repeatedly shown how the distribution of surplus produce in directions where it is presently scarce may give rise to indebtedness in the short term and mutual reliance in the longer term, laying the foundations of a relationship which it becomes in the interest of neither side to disrupt through quarrelling. The same principles may also be seen in operation in stock transactions under which larger herds are split up and the beasts placed in the care of presently less fortunate co-residents or kinsmen. They are also observable in the innumerable property transactions associated with marriage in different societies. Whether the property concerned consists of the valuable durables which pass in the course of bridewealth-type transactions, or in the perishables which pass repeatedly between the two sets of kin in the course of a marriage, the transactions can be seen as operating to strengthen ties between the groups concerned, making less likely the intrusion of a disruptive quarrel.

We noted in Chapter 5 how shaming and ridicule may be used in a nomadic community to bring a wrongdoer back into line through public exposure of his conduct.[3] This means of dealing with anti-social behaviour can, if anything, be even more effective in a small settled community where the exposed person has to face other members on a continual daily basis. We have also seen one form which such shaming may take in the door-step harangue, practised in the Goodenough Island community of Kalauna.[4] Young reports a further means of shaming on Goodenough, also found in other Melanesian

3. See pp. 88–90 above.
4. See p. 62 above.

communities, which involves the competitive exchange of surplus foodstuffs.[5] Under this procedure a man who has been wronged presents the wrongdoer with his largest and finest yam, or some other item of prestige food, intending to shame the latter by giving him something bigger and better than he is immediately able to pay back. The wrongdoer is forced to return the gesture, suffering humiliation if he has to respond with an inferior article, but escalating the conflict if, contrary to the donor's calculations, he is able to improve on the original gift. From the observer's position it is not immediately clear where the shame lies in receiving a handsome gift which seriously depletes the giver's resources and at the same time enhances the receiver's. But, according to Young, the actors themselves, fanatically keen and competitive gardeners, are satisfied about the shame-inducing qualities of this procedure, and about its efficacy as an institution of social control. The threat of one of these challenges, they believe, 'induces good, norm-oriented behaviour', and its being put into effect punishes the wrongdoer.[6]

This 'fighting with food', which Young argues has increased in importance under the European administration with the suppression of direct inter-personal violence, is not limited to the competitive exchange of single items of food by individuals. In its major form, *abutu*, it involves the wronged person and his immediate kinsmen and associates in assembling and preparing for transport large quantities of prestige foodstuffs, which the wrongdoer and his own kin must then attempt to match. As Young points out, this procedure seems an uncertain control mechanism in that the wrongdoer may well be able to improve on the original gift and thus make the quarrel worse. However, it appears that the challenge to *abutu* will not be made without careful calculation of resources by the challenger. Moreover, in the welter of produce that changes hands it will often appear to X that he has won because his yams are best, and to Y that he is the victor because his presentation of some

5. *Fighting with Food*, p. 125.
6. ibid., pp. 207–27.

other category of food is the more ample. At least in the case of the Kalauna, therefore, it seems that these transactions seldom result in escalation of the trouble.

One important aspect of these competitive exchanges as control mechanisms must lie in their diversionary value. Much energy is channelled into the task of collecting, measuring, packing and transporting the material for exchange, with the result that when it is all over few will be keen to begin again or embark on other forms of hostility too quickly. Malinowski implied this important diversionary element in his description of the closely related Trobriand *buritila' ulo*.[7] There he tells of the furious activity involved in collecting and checking the yams, and in preparing a container for transit, and notes the exhaustion of both sides once the exchange is complete.

While transfers of surplus material goods may thus play a cohesive role through creating and maintaining relationships between individuals and groups, it can be seen from Young's description of the *abutu* how easily similar transactions may have divisive consequences in providing the means through which quarrels may be pursued and struggles for power acted out. Early on Mauss showed in his famous *Essai sur le don*[8] how the seemingly gratuitous transfer or destruction of property could constitute a vehicle for establishing or maintaining political prestige and superiority. An example is provided by the 'potlatch' of the North American Kwakiutl Indians in which men seek to achieve and consolidate political ascendancy through the ostentatious destruction of valuable goods.[9]

The suggestion that fear of the gods, and of other mystical agencies, may operate to secure compliance with socially approved norms is found very widely in the literature of social anthropology. This is not surprising when it is remembered that in many societies most misfortunes are attributed either to some form of divine intervention, or to the practice of witchcraft and

7. *Coral Gardens and Their Magic*; see also p. 60 above.
8. Published as *The Gift* in an English translation by Cunnison.
9. Codère, *Fighting with Property*.

sorcery. Certainly, in many societies where arable farming is practised the success of the crop is seen as being in the lap of the gods, or at the mercy of sorcerers. Where divine beings are believed to have an immediate influence on the success of the harvest, elaborate rituals designed to please them often precede and accompany all major agricultural operations, and the quality of the crops may be held to depend on these rituals being properly carried out by competent persons. Beyond this, success may also hinge on the correct observance by all members of the community concerned of behavioural patterns pleasing to the gods. Thus, for example, it is reported from several African societies that if certain timber trees are cut during the ploughing season, hail will later fall and destroy the crop. Where beliefs such as these are held, fear that the crops will fail must to some extent ensure that approved norms of conduct in the area concerned are complied with.

Fear of sorcery may operate in the same way. In some Melanesian societies, for example, it is believed that a crop can be ruined by sorcery, and that the power to inflict this harm is available to most adults.[10] These beliefs lead to elaborate efforts being made to 'doctor' gardens in such a way as to protect them from mystical attack, and attempts to avoid any action which might provoke sorcery in retaliation. The gardener will also take care to show special politeness towards anyone who might bear him ill-will. When a poor crop does materialize, he will then rack his brains to remember whom in the community his conduct can possibly have offended; if he can think of someone, he has the alternative of trying to make amends or embarking on some retaliatory sorcery himself. The importance of sorcery beliefs as control mechanisms should certainly not be minimized; but they are sources of trouble too, as is clear from some reports which describe communities heavy with gloom under the oppressive fear of sorcery, and the prodigious strains which the effort to be polite to everyone can impose.

The belief that illness and death, as well as material mis-

10. See, for instance, Malinowski, *Coral Gardens and Their Magic*; Young, *Fighting with Food*.

fortune, may be attributable to the work of humans ill-disposed towards the sufferer creates special problems of control in settled societies where members find themselves living together in continuing face-to-face contact. Such a belief, in postulating some human agency as the cause of these crises, is in itself almost inevitably a source of conflict, as it leads people to look around them in the community for the culprit whenever death or sickness strikes. Every society where these beliefs are found has its own means of handling the suspicions, accusations and quarrels which result from them; a neat one is that which Bohannan recorded in his book *Justice and Judgment among the Tiv*.[11] The Tiv, a patrilineal grouping from North Western Nigeria, hold that illness and death may be caused by the actions of humans who have certain inherent characteristics in their bodies known as *tsav*. The identity of the individual responsible for a particular death can be established by the deceased's kinsmen carrying out a Tiv ritual process, called the breaking of *swem*, following the decease. When *swem* has been broken, the person responsible will himself die, and a post-mortem reveals in his internal organs the substance, *tsav*, which marks him down as being responsible for the earlier death. Bohannan illustrates all this through the death of a Tiv called Geza. When Geza's sister died under unexplained circumstances, people wondered who was responsible, and feared that other members of the lineage might also be attacked, so they broke *swem* at her funeral. After a while, Geza himself fell ill and died, giving rise to the suspicion that he might have killed his sister. So Geza's chest was opened and in the heart was found the substance, *tsav*. This satisfied those performing the operation and others present that it was Geza who had been responsible for his sister's death. Everyone was then able to relax and other suspicions fell away. Now they all knew who had killed Geza's sister; and he was dead, so the danger was gone. Such a mechanism, in identifying a culprit who is both *outside* the living community and incapable of further action,

11. pp. 196–203.

has obvious advantages as a means of restoring peace among the survivors.

With settlement, some of the control mechanisms which we considered in the previous chapter thus retain their importance, especially those which operate to ensure continuing cooperation, to divert attention away from some quarrel, or to channel anger and blame away towards some external object. At the same time, others acquire a new emphasis or become less readily resorted to. Most important in this context is the loss of mobility which goes with arable farming, making dispersal a much less easy solution to conflict than it is for people who are likely to be on the move anyway. While crops have to be seen to, it is no longer possible to move away for a change of scene simply because a quarrel threatens. A dispute has to be resolved where it arises, in the context of continuing face-to-face relations, without the ready solution of immediate changes in group composition. It may also have to be dealt with fast if it is not to disrupt essential tasks in the often inflexible cycle of arable production. Such circumstances are likely to result in greater emphasis being placed on settlement-directed discussion, and upon the close regulation of fighting wherever this represents an accepted response to a wrong.

Settlement-directed talking offers disputants an opportunity to articulate their grievances, gives third parties a chance to guide them towards some agreed solution which is acceptable to both and at the same time reminds them of the values of harmony and cohesion. From almost all settled societies there are reports of third parties acting as go-betweens or bringing disputants together and guiding them towards some compromise, perhaps involving compensation or simply promises as to future conduct. As we saw in Chapter 4, settlement-directed discussion may take many different forms, depending on the values and organization of the society concerned; these will be considered in more detail in later chapters. Here we simply note the importance which such talk must assume if disputes are to be successfully dealt with in the context of a settled face-to-face community.

Sustained fighting within a small face-to-face community can be intolerably disruptive both of social relations between co-residents and of the essential tasks of making a living. Because of this, within most settled groups where direct inter-personal violence is an approved or tolerated mode of responding to a wrong its exercise is made subject to considerable limitations. This seems to be the case even in those societies where a man's honour is seen to demand an immediate and robust response to a wrong. We consider the form which such limitations may take in Chapter 7.

While hostile encounters *between* communities may not be so closely regulated, controls which have the effect of avoiding serious disruption of the business of making a living are widely reported. For example, the fighting may be called off once one or two people have been killed on either side; or periodic truces may be called.[12] Often such conventions are explicitly related to the exigencies of the harvest. Koch, writing about the Jale people of Highland New Guinea, states:[13]

> Since all belligerents need to harvest food, the principal parties to the conflict often agree on a temporary cessation to the fighting in a shouted exchange at the close of battle.
>
> After several weeks of intermittent skirmishes, anxiety that the long neglect of garden work will lead to famine militates against continuing open warfare. An indefinite extension of a harvesting recess then constitutes a kind of armistice. This truce is a rather perilous affair, because now small bands of men from the men's house of a victim whose death has not been revenged on the battlefield make occasional clandestine expeditions across the demarcation line in search of a chance to ambush an enemy. On these forays the raiders capture pigs from the foraging grounds of the hostile village if they perceive no risk of immediate discovery. Since a revenge action of this kind often leads to a resumption of open warfare, vengeance expeditions increase in frequency and audacity when new gardens are ready for harvest.

Where established mechanisms fail to resolve a dispute, or at least to bring it under such control that the everyday life of the

12. See, for example, Berndt, *Excess and Restraint*; Koch, *War and Peace in Jalemo*.

13. *War and Peace in Jalemo*, p. 77; see also pp. 116–17 below.

community can continue, some form of dispersal under which the disputants are physically separated represents an ultimate solution. In groups of hunters and gatherers, as we saw, this solution need not be one of last resort, and may be chosen in preference to any other as involving the least cost to the parties concerned. However, for disputants in a more sedentary context the disadvantages of break-up are potentially much greater. Immediate withdrawal may be ruled out where crops essential to the support of life are in the course of their growing cycle and have yet to be harvested. Even in the longer term, the use of more or less permanent dwellings and the acquisition of numerous items of property that are associated with a settled life may pose considerable logistic difficulties. In societies where there are shortages of good arable land the acquisition of fresh lands may also be problematic; and even where ample land is available new fields will almost certainly have to be pioneered from the bush. Notwithstanding these constraints, physical separation is reported from most societies as the ultimate means of dealing with a dispute between parties who are irrevocably at odds.

The readiness with which dispersal is resorted to and the form it takes must depend to some extent on the nature of the society concerned. In communities which practise shifting agriculture and have to move on anyway at relatively short intervals as the soil in a particular area becomes exhausted it may make relatively little difference whether a household moves to another site this year or next. Even where such a group holds together until a move is made essential on horticultural grounds, the occasion of the move will provide members of the community with an opportunity to get away from co-residents or kinsmen with whom tension has developed.

Instances of dispersal and continuous processes of re-grouping certainly should not be seen as exceptional in societies relying primarily on agricultural production. As we saw,[14] Turner has depicted fission as an inevitable part of the life-cycle of a Ndembu community. In these villages of shifting

14. On p. 47 above.

cultivators, the rivalries between men aspiring to future head-manship predictably lead to disputes as a result of which dis-appointed individuals go to live in other villages, or take away a segment of the existing community and pioneer a new settle-ment. Turner noted that trouble of this type typically reached a peak at a time when the community had to move elsewhere in search of fresh soil anyway, so the occasion of this move enabled the existing community to re-group more harmoniously until such time as the next struggle for the headmanship developed. While the ease of reorganization in the face of disharmony is certainly greatest in a society of shifting culti-vators, break-up as a solution to disputes is not peculiar to them. In societies settled more or less permanently on the same tract of land, a move may present greater problems, but such societies tend often to be made up of considerably larger groupings than those of shifting cultivators, with the result that people who do not get on with one another can be accom-modated even within the same community at a safe distance from each other. Even in some large, settled African chiefdoms fission is seen as an inevitable, though regrettable, feature of the development of the groupings of which the society is made up.

In this chapter and the previous one the focus has been upon hunter/gatherers and agriculturists, to the neglect of pastora-lists. In several respects the control implications of herding fall between those of the other two means of making a living. At first sight, herdsmen may seem more akin to hunters and gatherers than to arable farmers from the standpoint of social control. Particularly, they are often on the move, following their beasts to water and pasture. But even where herding is not combined with some form of arable activity (and often it is) it involves consequences which are largely absent in the case of hunters and gatherers, but which are shared with people who garden. While herding may involve frequent movement, this movement is dictated by the needs of the herds and cannot necessarily be adjusted to permit the tension-reducing dispersals which play an important part in dealing with disputes in some hunting and gathering groups. Furthermore, herding activities at once imply an elaborate rule-base and are likely to be associated with a much wider range of potential disputes than is the case with hunter/gatherers. In this context we should remember that the herds themselves provide a basis for complex property relations, while enduring rights over grazing and water resources frequently become associated with particular individuals or groups.

7

Stateless Societies

In the two preceding chapters the main emphasis was upon the implications which a particular means of making a living may have for maintaining order and handling disputes: What difference does it make whether the members of a society wander about in search of food or settle down and cultivate the soil? Little attention was paid in that context to the consequences of differing forms of social and political organization. We were not concerned, for example, with the ways in which the control mechanisms found in societies made up of small groups of undifferentiated kin might differ from those of large centralized states. Questions of that kind form the subject of this and the following chapter. The organizational forms found in the societies with which we are concerned are varied; and no detailed attempt at classification is made. For the present purposes a rough and ready distinction is drawn between those with some form of centralized governmental organization and those without it. We look first at the latter, stateless societies.

When we consider the general implications which the absence of state organization may have for the maintenance of order and the handling of disputes it is necessary to remember that there are in all societies important control mechanisms which have little to do with governmental organization, and which certainly do not depend for their effectiveness upon the kind of coercive force which state organs may bring to bear. We have already noted, for example, those relationships of reciprocal obligation which Malinowski observed as playing a critical part in securing order in the Trobriands.[1] What he identified and emphasized there undoubtedly constitutes an important, though

1. See pp. 38–9 above.

partial, element of control in any society; one which may perhaps acquire greater significance where state organization is absent. Similarly, in those societies where plural group membership results in the presence of cross-cutting ties of loyalty of the kind which Colson identified in the case of the Plateau Tonga, the interplay of such ties is likely to have important implications for the control of conflict.[2]

Despite the presence of such shared characteristics, without some form of centralized government under which favoured means of settling disputes may be imposed and the outcomes of those processes enforced, the approved means of handling disputes in stateless societies are extremely varied. In some societies it is recognized that quarrels *should* be resolved through talk rather than by fighting, ostracism or sorcery. In others no particular value is attached explicitly to talking but it may be used alongside other methods of handling disputes. Elsewhere different values prevail, demanding as a matter of honour some direct physical response to many types of wrong and resulting in the identification of conciliatory gestures with weakness. In the last case retaliatory violence may represent the likely reaction to a wrong, and where further injury is inflicted this may in turn lead to sustained fighting between kinsmen and co-residents of the principals.

Prior to their 'pacification' by Dutch and Australian administrations these last conditions apparently characterized numerous societies living in the New Guinea Highlands. The American anthropologist Koch describes such a group in his book *War and Peace in Jalemo*. The Jale people live in compact villages and make a living out of gardening and keeping pigs, their most prestigious form of property. Most villages embrace two or more small residential groups made up of a cluster of dwellings around a 'men's house'. Sometimes one of these sub-groups of co-residents consists of the members of a single patrilineage, but more often two or more agnatic segments live together in the group, the male members of each lineage sharing the men's house. Each men's house generally contains one or more 'big men', transitory leaders whose position depends on

2. See pp. 55–6 above.

their physical strength, assertiveness and success in building up and maintaining a good credit balance of pigs. Jale are aggressive people among whom a quarrel can easily flare up into a physical confrontation, but 'big men' seem to play little part in controlling disputes and such influence as they do enjoy is limited to the men's house group to which they belong. Talking seems neither a well-established nor a particularly approved means of resolving trouble, and significantly the Jale language does not contain a word for settlement-directed talk, apart from one which Koch translates as 'shouting match'. Within a men's house group disputes among agnates and other co-residents are to some extent regulated by the need to maintain the solidarity of the group sufficiently to protect shared political and economic interests. However, in disputes involving individuals from different groups or villages private violence can easily escalate into warfare between groups. The ensuing conflict seems restricted only by the common need to cultivate, the periodic necessity of combining against some larger hostile group, and the fear of the principals in the dispute that they will have to compensate their supporters for injuries inflicted on them in the course of the fighting.

It must not be assumed that in societies similar to the Jale, where quarrels among individuals may lead to fighting between groups, disputes are typically concluded with the rout and destruction of one side or the other following a period of unregulated combat. On the contrary, a majority of accounts describe highly formalized encounters in which fighting of a limited character takes place within a framework of mutually accepted conventions. The kinds of restriction with which fighting may be hedged about are well illustrated in Rappaport's account of the Maring people of New Guinea.[3] Like the Jale, Maring are divided up into numerous sub-groups, each of which occupies a defined territory and enjoys potentially hostile relations with similar groups in the surrounding area. Within

---

3. *Pigs for the Ancestors: Ritual in the Ecology of a New Guinea People*. The description here is in the present tense, although the situation which Rappaport writes of was brought to an end by contact with the Australian administration in the late 1950s.

each territorial unit there are typically several agnatic segment
cultivating more or less distinct areas of land but ready to
combine at any moment for defensive purposes against out
siders.

Maring see retaliatory violence as the appropriate response
to a wide range of wrongs, including taking a woman without
permission, killing someone else's pig or stealing crops. Where
death or serious injury results from such retaliation, this i
likely to end in fighting between the groups to which the parties
belong, because the victim's group see themselves as obliged to
avenge the injury against the community of the person directly
responsible. Such vengeance is appropriate whether those
immediately involved belong to different territorial units or to
separate segments within the same territory; but in the latter
case the matter is more likely to be resolved without fighting a
co-residents admonish the parties and persuade them that their
common interests transcend the immediate quarrel. Where
fighting does commence between two segments within a single
territory, other segments from the area may break up the fight
before further injury is inflicted.

These Maring encounters are highly formalized set-piece
battles, accompanied by elaborate ritual off the battlefield. The
exchange begins when members of the group sustaining the
injury shout out a challenge calling on the enemy to prepare
for a fight. A battle-ground is then chosen and clearing parties
from both sides strip the area of bush, taking care to avoid
direct contact in the course of these preparations. Once the
ground is ready, fighting takes place in two distinct stages. The
first, the 'nothing fight', is preceded by ritual preparation
designed to secure the protection of the ancestors and other
supernatural agencies. Then the two sides line up opposite each
other within bow-shot behind large shields and fire is exchanged
with arrows and throwing spears. These static encounters often
continue over a number of days, with the respective combatant
retiring at nightfall. Because both sides keep their distance and
light weapons are used, serious injuries or fatalities are seldom
sustained during the 'nothing fight'.

When the 'nothing fight' takes place between two segments occupying a single territory, it may be the full extent to which hostilities go. Tempers have an opportunity to cool during the set-piece exchange, less enthusiastic allies may damp down the martial ardour of the principals, or sufficient wounds may be inflicted by the side issuing the challenge to enable them to feel that the wrong has been redressed. Under such circumstances some kind of agreement may be reached in the course of shouted exchanges between the combatants themselves. Alternatively non-aligned neutrals may prevail on the combatants to desist. Rappaport describes occasions on which neutrals brought the fighting to an end by stoning the combatants or physically interspersing themselves between the battle lines.

If the hostilities do not cease with the 'nothing fight', the 'true fight' follows. After further extensive ritual preparations, the sides meet again on the battle-ground with axes and jabbing spears added to their equipment. On this occasion those in the front rank on each side stand toe to toe behind their shields, fighting individual duels, while those behind attempt to shoot down any enemies who show themselves. Where serious casualties are sustained this generally results from a man being felled by an arrow, enabling the opponent he is fighting to rush in and finish him off with axe or spear. But even in the 'true fight' a static battle might continue for weeks on end without decisive advantage to either side. Over this period intermissions are taken by agreement where essential gardening operations or unfavourable climatic conditions demand them. There is a further break whenever a fatality is inflicted while the necessary ritual procedures are undertaken.

Rappaport suggests that these set pieces typically continue until both sides feel there has been sufficient killing and a truce is then called. More rarely, the fighting is ended with a rout and dispersal of one side. This generally occurs where allies desert, leaving one side with an obvious numerical advantage which encourages them to break away from the set piece and overrun the enemy.

With the calling of a truce a sustained period of peace is

assured, for this sets in motion a lengthy ritual cycle in the course of which supernatural agencies and the allies are rewarded for their help in the fighting. The successful conclusion of this cycle in a year-long festival, the *Kaiko*, necessitates a massive build-up in the pig population which, according to Rappaport's observations, can scarcely take less than five years. A rule recognized by all the Maring communities forbids any group to recommence hostilities before it has completed this cycle.

The dominant impression of these Maring encounters is of the controls with which they are hedged about and of the limited extent to which they interfere with essential processes in everyday life. The restricted nature of the fighting is plain in Rappaport's accounts of carefully staged set pieces, and of the clearly defined steps through which the fighting must pass. Indeed he suggests that we should see the 'nothing fight' as 'a debate, held in a setting that minimizes the danger of casualties while satisfying martial imperatives, between those eager to fight and those hoping to preserve the peace'.[4] The controlled character of these exchanges is also clear from the extent to which fighting is subordinated to essential agricultural activities. These restrictions, together with the lengthy periods of peace required for compliance with ritual procedures, not only provide ample time for tempers to cool but ensure that such fighting as does take place remains of a limited and undisruptive nature. This Maring example thus shows how fighting as a means of resolving disputes may be as closely regulated in some societies as settlement-directed talking may be in others, and how fighting between groups need not imply destructive warfare in which one side conquers or annihilates the other.

Societies in which retaliatory violence represents an approved response are not confined to Melanesia. For example, Evans-Pritchard describes precariously established means of controlling inter-personal violence within a face-to-face community and continuing, if sporadic, fighting between neighbouring communities of the same ethnic group when he writes about

4. ibid., p. 123

he pastoral Nuer of the Southern Sudan.[5] Nuer are fiercely
aggressive and for them the approved response to many kinds
of wrong is immediate retaliatory violence. Because of this,
face-to-face discussion is seldom feasible when a dispute arises
even where the disputants live in the same village and are
members of the same lineage. Even once the incident in question has passed, there is little possibility of the disputants and
their respective kinsmen sitting down together and talking
about the matter, as further violence is still likely to ensue.
However, Nuer do recognize that normal life becomes impossible within a small face-to-face community when some of the
members are likely to spear each other on sight, and accept that
the payment of material compensation can remove the threat
of retaliation. But this has to be arranged by mediators who
pass backwards and forwards between the respective disputants
and their kinsmen while the elements of a compromise are
constructed, rather than through face-to-face negotiation.
According to Evans-Pritchard, this mediation is usually carried
out by a Nuer ritual specialist, the 'leopardskin chief'. The
possibility of his arranging a compromise before a dispute
escalates into further violence is improved by the fact that a
wrongdoer may seek sanctuary with him and is immune from
attack so long as he stays in the leopardskin chief's homestead.
Once this respite has been achieved, the leopardskin chief visits
the wronged man and his kin, begging them to accept compensation for the wrong rather than actively pursue the quarrel
once the wrongdoer leaves the sanctuary. Thereafter he moves
between the two groups, carrying messages and exercising his
own persuasion, until agreed compensation is arranged. Outside a group of close kinsmen and co-residents, such a negotiated solution is very difficult to achieve and a killing, injury or
other serious wrong may be the source of sporadic fighting for
generations between the groups of kin involved. For Nuer,
fighting and killing are manly occupations, and honour demands
that wrongs shall be avenged.

*

5. *The Nuer.*

As the Nuer example shows, the absence of centralized political organization does not necessarily imply that talking will not be resorted to as a means of resolving disputes; and we shall see that in some other acephalous societies this represents the dominant and approved mode. But the absence of state agencies does have implications both for the *form* which settlement-directed talking is likely to take, and for the means through which the outcome of such processes is secured. Particularly important in this context are the implications for third-party intervention. Wherever third parties intervene in trying to resolve a dispute, the same questions arise: Where are they to be drawn from? How does their intervention acquire legitimacy? Around what institutions in the society will the dispute-settlement processes in which they participate be organized? At least on one level these questions are simply answered in the case of a society with state organization, because that organization will in all probability identify officials with authority to settle disputes. However, the answers are much less straightforward in the case of an acephalous society, and must depend in part on the particular organizational forms found within it. In a community consisting simply of a group of undifferentiated kinsmen, the basis for intervention may be founded upon age, closeness of kinship, or upon some individually acquired attribute (such as being recognized as a 'big man' or having shown particular skill in dealing with disputes in the past). In an acephalous society with more complex institutions, such as those of lineage, age-set or caste, position within one of these sub-systems may identify the person to intervene in a particular dispute. Furthermore, such a sub-system may itself provide the institutional framework and arena within which the dispute settlement process takes place.

The presence of sub-systems like age-sets and lineages in some acephalous societies gives an indication of the wide variety of organizational forms found in such societies and at the same time points to a key attribute whereby dispute-settlement processes in some of these societies can be distinguished. In contrast to the position in a community consisting simply of an undifferentiated aggregate of kin, where such sub-systems are present they introduce important elements of *choice* into the process. Such choice may extend in several directions and include: the reservoir of support that a particular disputant may turn to; the values and norms he may invoke in pursuing his cause; and the agency before which he takes the dispute for settlement. The implications of these areas of choice will be considered later in this chapter when dispute-settlement processes in the context of simpler organizational forms have been examined.

Processes of settlement-directed talking in a society without very complex institutional arrangements have been excellently described by Gulliver in his work on the Ndendeuli.[6] As we have already noted, an Ndendeuli community is made up of groups of undifferentiated kinsmen and affines. Within each community the members of individual households rely heavily on each other for cooperation in making a living. The most essential form of cooperation relates to the process of clearing and preparing the fields for sowing, and fencing the cleared land to keep animals away from the crops during the growing season. Although these Ndendeuli communities are generally formed by a man of particular skill and initiative who goes off with some kinsmen to pioneer a new stretch of bush, they lack any form of centralized government and even during his lifetime the founder is not in any sense a ruler.

In the event of a dispute arising between two members of an Ndendeuli community, the approved method of dealing with it is for the disputants to meet together with their kinsmen for settlement-directed discussion. Third parties, who in the nature of these communities will inevitably be kinsmen or affines of the disputants, must in theory play one of two roles. They may join either disputant as a supporter (Gulliver describes such people as members of a disputant's 'action-set'), or stand aside and purport to perform a mediatory function in a more or less impartial way. Gulliver found that the action-sets were built up of people with whom the disputants enjoyed the closest ties

6. *Neighbours and Networks.*

of material cooperation (e.g. if A has repeatedly helped B in his clearing and hoeing operations, and *vice versa*, either will expect the support of the other in the event of a dispute). Each disputant will try to secure as members of his action-set people who are influential in the community and who are listened to with respect in a meeting: sheer numbers, while important, may be matched by quality. Mediators, on the other hand, are likely to be drawn from people with whom neither party has particularly close ties of cooperation and who stand equidistant from each in terms of kinship. Outright support in the event of a dispute strengthens the ties between the supporter and the disputant, and necessarily leads to a corresponding cooling of relations with the other party. Similarly, while successful mediation can increase prestige in the community, failure to achieve a settlement, or demonstrated partiality for one side, will be damaging. Because of this, in a small community third parties have to calculate very carefully the consequences of a particular position or alignment and judge nicely the degree of support they may extend. Each dispute leaves its mark on the community in the sense that new loyalties are established and old ones decline. Existing hostilities are similarly liable to modification.

Once a meeting has been convened, both sides outline their version of the dispute, and the competing assertions and demands will be supported by the respective action-sets. As the overall picture becomes clear, those who have adopted a neutral posture hitherto may suggest possible lines of settlement, urging both parties to give ground in such a way that their respective positions converge to a point where some agreed outcome is possible. In doing so they necessarily put a given construction on events and implicitly allocate responsibility for the dispute. At this point the supporters of each disputant may themselves urge a particular compromise and outline the merits of some course of action which a mediator has proposed. In this way a solution can speedily be reached, and the meeting end successfully. But equally the meeting may break up with the rival positions hardened in deadlock. Where this happens, another meeting has to be arranged to try again. While each disputant retains a degree of independence, once the meeting begins and his action-set has been convened he is to some extent constrained by the opinions the members express and the courses of action they favour. If influential members of the set favour a particular solution by way of settlement, and advocate it strongly, there is little the disputant can do but accept this, for otherwise his group of supporters will simply melt away if the meeting ends without a conclusion. Certainly where members of the respective action-sets are as one as to the solution to be followed, there is little that the principals can do but comply.

In searching for a settlement, reference may be made to socially accepted rules, to the importance of sustaining particular social ties and to the harmony of the community as a whole. While appeal to some Ndendeuli norm must underlie any claim which one party may make against the other and may form the criteria on which a settlement is urged, such norms tend to be general and ill-defined, rather than detailed and clear-cut. This lack of clarity is illustrated in the norms relating to bridewealth and to the behaviour of the son-in-law. While Ndendeuli are clear that bridewealth must be presented in marriage, and that a good son-in-law has a duty to give material help to his wife's father, the rules do not make it clear what constitutes an adequate presentation of bridewealth, what is sufficient help to a father-in-law, or where these different responsibilities begin and end in relation to each other. The uncertainty of these Ndendeuli norms thus provides ground over which argument can range if a quarrel between a man and his son-in-law should arise.

Besides any socially approved norms which may be specifically relevant to a dispute a higher appeal may also be made to the parties that they must patch up the dispute in the interests of harmony in the group. Such an appeal will run: 'We are all kinsmen; we cannot allow this quarrel to continue and disrupt our lives.' A call like this will take on particular urgency if the quarrel persists, or if it occurs at a time when its prosecution delays vital agricultural activities.

Beyond any such appeals to norms and underlying values political undercurrents will also be present. The 'big man', able to form a large action-set made up of the men who are influential in the community and articulate in debate, will be well placed to achieve the more favourable settlement.

These attributes of the Ndendeuli dispute-settlement processes are vividly illustrated by a dispute between a man and his son-in-law which Gulliver recounts.[7] Rajabu, returning home from a period of migrant labour, gave his father-in-law, Sedi, a present of a blanket and some cloth. Sedi at first seemed satisfied with the gift, but later demanded of Rajabu a further instalment of bridewealth, which the latter refused. In the course of the dispute it transpired that Rajabu had given a large part of the money he had brought back with him to a kinsman, Musa, who had helped Rajabu with earlier bridewealth instalments. Musa was himself being pressed for bridewealth payments by his own father-in-law, Yasini. It seems it was only when Sedi heard what Rajabu had given to Musa that he himself made further claims. When Rajabu rejected Sedi's claim, Sedi decided to call a meeting to press the matter. In doing so he called on an influential man in the community, Konga, who was equally closely related to himself and Rajabu's father Zadiki (Konga was Sedi's father's sister's son, and Zadiki's father's brother's son). Konga suggested that a meeting be held at his house, and both sides set about recruiting groups of supporters.

At the meeting Sedi asserted that he wanted more bridewealth, without specifying how much. Zadiki responded by saying that Rajabu had paid enough, and then outlined what had been given, thus implying that this was an acceptable amount. He also suggested that what Sedi was asking for was not further bridewealth, but a larger share of Rajabu's savings from work. He answered this demand by outlining Rajabu's history of generosity on previous occasions. Neither talked explicitly about rules, but confined themselves to statements of fact. Speakers from both groups of supporters then followed.

7. *Neighbours and Networks*, pp. 145–51.

When people on both sides had spoken, the 'big man' who had called the meeting, Konga, said he thought that perhaps Rajabu should have given more to Sedi when he got back from work. He then asked Yasini if he would be prepared to accept a smaller instalment of bridewealth from Musa. Yasini agreed to this, making it very difficult for Rajabu to persist in his argument that he had no more to give to Sedi. Further talk followed, and ultimately Rajabu agreed to give Sedi a further sum of 25s. This money was handed over, Sedi promised that he would make no further claims to bridewealth against Rajabu, and the matter ended in the communal drinking of beer.

The consequences which this form of organization has for the Ndendeuli processes of dispute settlement appear clearly in this account and in the case history. First are the limitations imposed upon third parties where they have no authority to impose a decision on the disputants. This lack of authority is underlined in instances which Gulliver cites of meetings frequently breaking up without any conclusion having been reached. Such a conclusion is only reached when the disputants themselves, however reluctantly, agree upon one. Therefore the role of third parties cannot extend beyond helping to achieve that agreement. They do this, first, by constituting a forum within which discussion may take place; secondly, as members of the respective action-sets, by formulating the positions of the two sides; and, thirdly, by building, as Konga did in the illustration, the elements of a compromise out of the positions which develop. Analytically, the role of the action-set member, and that of the mediator are distinct in this process; and in their nature they will be performed by different people. But mediators are not necessarily without bias, as Konga's behaviour in Rajabu's case showed. Further, members of the respective action-sets, as well as any mediator, may play a significant part in edging the respective positions closer and, finally, articulating the possible solutions implicit in the positions which have been worked out. Nor should the influence of third parties in achieving a settlement be under-emphasized, for, although they lack any decision-making power, their assessment of what constitutes an appropriate compromise will be hard for the parties to resist, particularly if a consensus develops between the two sets, or if a preponderance of political muscle is lined up on one side or the other. No disputant can afford to hold out for a solution which his supporters do not favour, as in doing so he may lose the possibility of cooperation valuable to him on later occasions.

A second general point, which emerges clearly in Rajabu's case, is the flavour of bargain and compromise inherent in this settlement process. As the outcome must lie in agreement, the formula will be found in the most which each party is prepared to concede and the least he is prepared to accept. Under such conditions norms cannot be exclusive determinants of an outcome, and considerations such as the respective economic strength and political muscle of the different parties become important. But so far as the part played by Ndendeuli norms in the process is concerned, Gulliver argues that their very lack of clarity is of vital importance. This characteristic introduces an element of flexibility which provides leeway for successful negotiation. Were the rules clear-cut, one avenue of compromise would be unavailable.

These Ndendeuli communities, consisting as they do of small autonomous groups of undifferentiated kinsmen within which no sharp divisions are drawn on the basis of age, represent a relatively simple organizational form. Much more complex arrangements may be found in some acephalous societies. The shape which these complexities may take and their implications for settlement-directed talking are well illustrated through the Arusha, another East African society that Gulliver has exhaustively described.[8] The Arusha are settled agriculturalists who live on the slopes of Mount Meru in Northern Tanzania. Like the Ndendeuli they lack any form of centralized government, but the society is made up of considerably more complex components than the simple groups of undifferentiated kin that characterize an Ndendeuli community.

8. *Social Control in an African Society.*

All Arusha claim membership of one of a number of patrilineal descent groups, each founded by one of the male pioneer
settlers in their present territory (who arrived there about
1830). But unlike the case in many societies with a strong
lineage organization, lineage membership and residential grouping do not coincide. Instead, the homesteads of members of a
given lineage are likely to be scattered around all over Arusha
country rather than clustered together in a discrete group. As
well as claiming membership of a patrilineage, each Arusha
male also belongs to an age-set, into which he is admitted with
others of his generation following initiation. As the members of
a given set grow older, they pass through four distinct stages,
each associated with particular kinds of work and responsibility
within the society.

Arusha do not live in well-defined villages, but in homesteads
located here and there across the arable lands which they keep
under cultivation. These lands are also divided up into a
number of geographical units which Gulliver describes as
'parishes'. Thus any Arusha male belongs to a particular
lineage, is a member of a given age-set and lives in one of the
parishes into which the territory is divided. Strong ties of loyalty
and mutual responsibility are meant to bind a man to other
members of his lineage and to his age-mates, and although the
ties between co-residents in a given parish seem less close, such
residents do recognize themselves as a corporate group to the
extent of meeting together to discuss matters of common
interest which arise within the parish.

The presence of these three distinct sub-groupings in Arusha
society has important consequences in the event of a dispute
in that they define reservoirs of support for those involved in a
quarrel and provide a choice of forum before which disputes
can be taken. So far as the recruitment of support is concerned,
the Arusha disputant can turn to members of his lineage and
to his age-mates for support simply *because* they are members
of his lineage or his age-mates. Co-membership of these groupings in itself carries these obligations. In this respect there is a
sharp contrast with the Ndendeuli disputant, who may turn

only to those members of the community with whom he has succeeded, through cooperation, in building up ties of reciprocal obligation, thus making a man's skill, energy and influence in the community the main determinants of the support he can rely on. While these factors are also important in the Arusha context, they coexist there with other sources of support inherent in the structure of the society. The presence of plural reservoirs of support in itself gives an Arusha disputant greater strategic freedom than his Ndendeuli counterpart.

The organization of Arusha society similarly ensures that a range of different agencies are available in the event of a dispute. Whereas among the Ndendeuli other members of the community to which a man belongs provide a single forum to which he can appeal in search of a settlement, an Arusha disputant can take his grievance before members of his parish, his lineage or his age-set. This possibility of choice is of great importance as it enables him to air his problem in the forum where he believes his support is strongest; but Arusha values do impose some limitations upon the freedom with which a forum can be chosen. According to these values trouble among members of a lineage should be kept *within* the lineage and a similar sentiment is expressed so far as age-mates are concerned. It goes with this idea of 'privacy' to the group that disputes between members of a single lineage should be taken to a meeting of the lineage, rather than to either of the other two agencies, and that quarrels between age-mates should be similarly settled within the set to which they belong. Only where two members of the same parish are in dispute who are neither age-mates nor members of the same lineage does the parish meeting constitute the approved venue for discussion. The guidelines imposed by this notion of privacy to the group are not invariably followed, as Gulliver's material shows; but the principle constitutes an important consideration in the process of choosing a forum.

Even in our own society the idea of law processes working themselves through according to fixed rules towards an inevitably determined end provides a distorted view of the procedures in which the litigants themselves make crucial choices as a dispute unfolds. In the Arusha case the presence of parallel agencies gives the exercise of litigant choice an even more crucial bearing upon the outcome of the proceedings. To some extent the nature and location of a disputant's supporters will govern the forum to which he will wish ideally to take the dispute. If he is assured of the support of influential members of his lineage, the lineage provides the best forum; if his lineage and age-set are strong within his parish, the parish meeting will be favoured and so on. But the nature of the dispute will also be important. Each of these main sub-groups of Arusha society has its own socially approved rules, and within these groups different emphasis will be given to rules which enjoy common acceptance within the society as a whole. Accordingly, a disputant who wishes to emphasize rules associated with lineage solidarity in his argument will be likely to seek to have the matter heard within the lineage. Correspondingly, the nature of the forum before which an Arusha dispute comes to be heard will have a significant bearing upon the criteria which are likely to be invoked by the disputant.

The socially accepted norms of Arusha society are freely articulated by Arusha in the context of a dispute. These norms, which in many areas are clear-cut and very detailed, typically form the basis of debate as a case is argued and are seen as having a considerable influence upon the outcome, even though they are not decisive. Further, they may exist on very different levels of specificity, ranging from broad abstract principles to detailed substantive rules. These norms can be invoked in such a way as to conflict, and where such conflict arises, much may depend on the forum in which the dispute is being argued out. Gulliver provides a telling illustration in Kadume's case.[9] Kadume's father had died while Kadume was still a child, and one of the father's fields had passed under the control of a paternal uncle, Soine. When Kadume was a grown man he demanded this field back to use himself. According to Arusha norms, this was a reasonable demand, as a son inherits his

9. *Social Control in an African Society*, p. 255.

father's land in preference to more remote members of the patrilineage. However, Soine refused to give up the field, arguing that Kadume had sufficient land of his own. As Kadume and his uncle were members of the same lineage, this grouping constituted the forum to which the dispute was taken. Kadume and those who supported him argued that he was entitled to the field as the deceased's son. Their opponents stressed that Kadume had sufficient land and that a quarrel like this among members of the same lineage was unseemly. Eventually a compromise was negotiated under which half the land concerned was returned to Kadume and the other half retained by Soine. Before this agreement was achieved men on both sides had argued that a peaceful solution should be reached in order to restore the harmony of the lineage, and Gulliver suggests that this consideration was a powerful factor in the acceptance of a compromise by both sides. Thus in this case a specific rule relating to the devolution of property within a lineage gives way to a more general principle concerned with the unity of the grouping. In this respect the forum in which the dispute came to be argued was crucial, as outside a meeting of co-members of a lineage arguments concerning the cohesion and harmony of this grouping would have been far less compelling.

Like the Ndendeuli processes already considered, this dispute was resolved through compromise in the absence of any authority in a position to impose and enforce a decision. But the process of settlement is different in two major respects. First, the necessary leeway for negotiation is achieved through a different means. In the Ndendeuli case, imprecision of norms provides the needed flexibility. Here there is no lack of clarity: the rule that a man inherits his father's field is crisp and unambiguous. It is the fact that the norms are seen as negotiable, as bargaining counters in the process of reaching an outcome, that provides the necessary flexibility to achieve a solution. Secondly, the mode of settlement is different. In the Ndendeuli case, a purportedly neutral mediator stands between the respective groups of supporters and helps guide them to a negotiated solution; here the initiative towards compromise comes from within the opposed groups themselves. This feature again has to do with the Arusha lineage organization. Arusha lineages are constructed in such a way that they divide into two all the way down, with the result that in the event of conflict arising within the lineage, each member knows on which side his support is due.[10] Obviously he has discretion to exert himself strongly or remain in the background; but the side he is on in any conflict within the lineage is decided for him in the principles of lineage organization. Thus, within the lineage there is no one who *can* stand in an intermediate position and behave as a neutral mediator. Further, as we have already noted, there is the principle of privacy to the group which operates strongly in lineage affairs. So only in the very last resort could someone from *outside* the lineage be drawn in to mediate.

In these two acephalous societies, one exhibiting very simple organizational forms and the other more complex ones, dispute-settlement procedures shared several similar features. In both cases face-to-face, settlement-directed talk constitutes the approved mode of settlement, while strong disapproval attaches to self-help. Both processes also have an overtly political flavour. Because there are no third parties recognized as having authority to resolve a dispute by decision, settlement has to be by compromise reached through negotiation. But despite these similarities, there are important differences. First, on account of Arusha social organization, and because of the value attached by Arusha to privacy within a group, in a significant number of disputes there can be no third party capable of occupying a bridging position and mediating between the two disputants. Yet, according to Gulliver's data, the absence of third parties in a mediatory role does not seriously impede settlement. The initiative in reaching a compromise solution comes instead from *within* the respective groups of supporters. A further difference lies in the much greater clarity of Arusha norms when contrasted with those of the Ndendeuli. At first sight this might be anticipated to impede the process of negotia-

10. ibid., pp. 134–40.

tion, as the necessary leeway cannot be found in the uncertainty of norm as it is in the Ndendeuli case. But instead the required flexibility lies in the way in which Arusha see their norms, as bargaining counters rather than as determinants of an outcome. Another important difference lies in the element of choice inherent in the more complex Arusha organization. Notwithstanding some constraints the Arusha disputant can often choose between three distinct reservoirs of support, manipulate the rules of three different sub-systems, and enjoy the possibility of raising a dispute before three parallel agencies – the lineage, the age-set and the parish.

The examples we have considered in this chapter show clearly that well-established means of handling conflict may be present in societies without centralized government. This point is as evident in the formalized combat of the Maring as it is in the settlement-directed talk of the Arusha. Nonetheless, in the absence of some authority empowered to make a decision and capable of enforcing it, political, military and economic strength represent important factors in the outcome of a dispute. The party who can command the largest and most powerful group of supporters within the community is as well placed on the battlefield as he is in the processes of settlement-directed talk.

In all of the societies examined the absence of state organization has its most important implications for the way in which third parties are able to intervene in someone else's quarrel. Although this does not mean that settlement processes – whether they involve fighting or talking – are limited to bilateral exchanges, the mode of intervention is restricted. Either they may align themselves in support of one or other of the disputants, taking his side in the fighting or talking; or they may occupy a neutral position, mediating or physically restraining the embattled parties. Under almost any organizational arrangements the first of these postures may be adopted; but as we saw earlier in this chapter the latter may be problematic under certain conditions.[11] Even where both are possible either may be hazard-

11. See p. 133 above.

ous, as in many small-scale societies third parties will either be so closely identified with one disputant through ties of kinship or cooperation as to be unable to take up a neutral stance with any credibility; or they may be closely associated with both, making it impossible to align with either without risking the breach of some valued relationship. The divided loyalties which arise in the latter circumstances may, as we noted earlier, in themselves reduce the level of a quarrel.[12]

Despite the fact that agencies with independent authority to resolve disputes are lacking in these societies, this does not necessarily remove the possibility of third party decision-making; it still lies within the power of the parties themselves to submit their quarrel by agreement to a third party for decision. Instances of stateless societies where such a procedure is followed, as opposed to some form of mediatory process, are rare in the anthropological literature; but they are to be found. According to Lewis, for example, an approved mode of settlement among nomadic Somali herdsmen is to submit disputes for decision to men chosen by disputants for their knowledge and impartiality.[13] These men hear out both sides and their witnesses, and then announce a decision which they urge both parties to accept with good grace. Whether such a decision 'sticks' depends on whether both parties feel the judgement to be fair, on their eagerness to have the matter settled and the pressure which their respective kinsmen and associates can bring to bear upon them. Even if the decision is not accepted, its outcome will clearly provide an important bargaining counter in subsequent negotiations.

The limitations which the absence of state organization imposes on the manner in which third parties intervene in a dispute also has implications for the part which may be played by rules. Where no-one has power to impose and enforce a decision, the socially accepted rules of the group concerned cannot determine the outcome of the dispute with the crisp simplicity that is theoretically possible where you have an

12. See pp. 55–6 above.
13. *A Pastoral Democracy*, pp. 229–34.

adjudicator and enforcement agencies. So long as the solution has to be reached through bilateral or mediatory processes, there must be flexibility in rule application, otherwise the leeway essential to bring the parties together is absent. The rigid application of rules typically leads, as we see in our own judicial system, to a situation in which one party wins and the other loses at the end of the day. Rules in acephalous societies must rather be seen as guidelines which third parties may invoke in shaping the negotiations, and bargaining counters in the hands of the disputants themselves. Because rules cease to be decisive under these conditions, the likelihood that other criteria will assume central importance is enhanced.

The lack of official agencies capable of directly enforcing a solution to a dispute once one has been reached is a feature common to all stateless societies. The absence emphasizes the importance which must be attached to achieving a settlement acceptable to both parties, or at least to so many other members of the community that departure from it by either party is made impracticable. A lack of the enforcement agencies found in societies with some form of state organization may also mean, as we saw in the Maring example, that much of the burden of securing an outcome once reached has to be carried in the ritual sphere. In many other stateless societies the conclusion of a dispute will be marked by elaborate feasting, the invocation of ancestors as witnesses or some other ceremonial procedure.

8
The State

The kinds of societies considered in Chapter 7 share at least one characteristic in that they lack a ruler, someone with supreme authority in whose name decisions touching the public affairs of the whole society may be taken and who claims obedience from all the members. These societies are not necessarily leaderless. It may be, for example, that groupings will temporarily form around particularly skilled and influential individuals and that within certain kinds of kinship groups those in a genealogically senior position can have an important say in the affairs of the group as a whole; but there is no-one recognized as having authority to make decisions concerning the general arrangements of the group, holding an office which devolves from one person to another according to socially accepted rules. Such a form of organization has important consequences for the way in which order is maintained in the society concerned; and these are considered in this chapter.

Societies with a recognizable state organization differ greatly, both in the details of their governmental arrangements and in the matter of size (in early nineteenth-century Africa there were states with populations which probably exceeded a million and others made up of just a few thousand people); but all share certain characteristics. One of these is the presence of a supreme authority, ruling over a defined territory, who is recognized as having power to make decision in matters of government (touching at least defence and the public services), is able to enforce such decisions and generally maintain order within the state. Thus, capacity to exercise coercive authority is a crucial ingredient: 'the ultimate test of a ruler's authority is ...

whether he possesses the power of life and death over his subjects'.[1]

The presence of this authority is further associated with the idea of continuity of office and the recognition of principles to determine how the office of ruler devolves from one person to another. The office may be hereditary, subject to some form of divine appointment, or elective; the point is that the ruler is not simply one of those 'big men' or notables who rise temporarily to positions of prominence in a community by virtue of wealth or some particular skill, without passing this position on to some defined successor as he grows old or the skill fails.

Another characteristic of all states is that on account of their relative size the ruler can scarcely exercise his authority directly upon all his subjects; powers are delegated to intermediaries standing between the ruler and the individual member. In many instances these intermediaries can roughly be divided into two categories, although these may overlap and the distinction have greater or lesser clarity. First, there will be those who directly surround the ruler, to whom he may delegate some of his decision-making powers, who may advise him and control access to him. Secondly, there will be those working at a local level, transmitting decisions made in the ruler's name and carrying them out, as well as perhaps making decisions in local matters on his behalf. These functions will at least involve organizing defence against external enemies, running the public services, collecting wealth and organizing labour for the maintenance of these and securing order in accordance with the approved values of the ruler. Depending on the size and organization of the state, the links in the chain of intermediaries between the ruler and the individual member will be fewer or more numerous. Overall, 'the larger, more heterogeneous and complex the state is, the more elaborate the ancillary machinery of government'.[2]

A majority of states possess two other characteristics, although these seem not to be universal. One of these is that quite

1. Lewis, *Social Anthropology in Perspective*, p. 315.
2. ibid., p. 313.

sharp divisions in terms of status and wealth are likely to be present; separating, perhaps, royals and commoners, and commoners and serfs. Alongside these divisions and frequently co-terminous with them may be found different ethnic groupings within a single state. Most, but not all, states seem to have embraced elements of more than one ethnic group. Typically, there will be a single dominant group to which others have become attached for protection or through the process of conquest. Such a pattern has been observed so widely that it has sometimes been argued that state organization invariably develops *through* the process of conquest; but the few examples of states consisting of a single grouping cast doubt on this theory.

This form of organization must necessarily have a significant effect upon the way in which order is maintained and disputes are settled. Inevitably, to a greater or lesser extent depending on the reach of the ruler's authority, the values held by the ruler will underlie and be reflected in the approved norms of conduct according to which everyday life in the state proceeds. The ruler will be in a position to formulate these rules explicitly if he chooses to do so, both in the context of disputes which come before him and in the form of more generalized pronouncements. A ruler is in theory in a position to 'legislate' by expressly affirming or changing a given rule, although legislative action seems to have been rather rare in the case of most states for which accounts exist.[3] Something more will be said later in this chapter about one case in which legislative action by rulers has been reported.

Notwithstanding the scarcity of what we would recognize as legislation, the socially accepted rules within societies with state organization tend to be clearly articulated and expressed in considerable detail. The need for this to be the case is understandable where groupings within the state have been absorbed through the process of conquest. Such groups, whose values

3. One exceptional account is that of Schapera, *Tribal Legislation among the Tswana of the Bechuanaland Protectorate*.

might differ considerably from those of the dominant group at the time of conquest, can be aided through the process of absorption by clear-cut formulation of the norms representing the values of the society of which they are to become a part. In respect of these groups, clarity of norms must also have importance for the purposes of enforcement.

Beyond this, the ruler is in a position, either directly or through intermediaries, to intervene in disputes in a way that would be impossible in the societies that have so far been considered. There we saw how third parties could generally adopt only a mediatory position and hope to guide the disputants to an outcome through compromise. Exceptionally third parties might act as arbitrators when called upon to decide a matter by the disputants themselves; but there was never anyone who could intervene on the authority of his office to *impose a decision* on the disputants from a third-party standpoint. The ruler, however, is in a position to do this. Without suggesting that there need be any notion of the separation of powers which characterizes our governmental arrangements, he may act in a manner closely analogous to the judge in our legal system. Linked to this decision-making power, and essential to it, is the power to enforce any decision which he reaches, as he will have available a military/police organization to carry out the decision by physical force. This capacity to adopt a judicial posture in the context of a dispute does not mean that a ruler will necessarily use it. As we shall see later, he may in practice resolve disputes through mediatory procedures like those already considered. What, however, is present with the development of state organization is the *potential* for making enforceable decisions from a third-party standpoint.

The presence of a ruler with power to make a decision takes away some of the constraints upon the range of criteria available in resolving a dispute. Where, in the absence of an adjudicator, a settlement has to be reached in the last resort through negotiatory procedures, the solution arrived at must be broadly acceptable to both parties if it is to be adhered to. There must also be a flexible approach towards the application of rules if the necessary leeway for negotiation is to be present. In theory, at least, the adjudicator is released from these constraints and may impose a decision on any basis that he thinks fit. He may reach a decision by purporting to make a rigid application of the rules, much in the way that the judicial process in a common law court is ideally seen to work; or he may decide a case in accordance with his own notions of fairness in the individual circumstances of the case, irrespective of the substance of any socially accepted norms; or he may hand down an entirely arbitrary *ad hoc* decision according to a momentary whim. Obviously there are difficulties for the adjudicator in making a decision that is not seen to be fair by the parties themselves: he will have to work hard to enforce it; there may be continuing hostility between the individuals or groupings concerned; and (if he does it often) his legitimacy will suffer over time. But, in the short term, an adjudicator can deal with a dispute in any way he pleases, provided he is backed up by the necessary force to impose it. Gulliver has put forward the hypothesis that, in general, rules are likely to be much more prominent in determining the outcome of a dispute where the process is adjudicatory than where it is negotiatory.[4] The rather limited material that is available suggests that he may be correct in this, but there is no necessary reason why an adjudicator should resolve disputes in accordance with rules. In some senses he has more freedom than the mediator who, without authority to decide, may have an even greater need for the backing of socially accepted rules in feeling his way towards an outcome acceptable to both parties.

In another sense the adjudicator typically has greater constraints imposed upon him in making a decision than the mediator. In many cases the mediator is a member of the small face-to-face community to which the two disputants belong. As such, he probably knows much about the overall background to the dispute, the relations between the disputants and other members of the community, and the long-term effect that

4. 'Case Studies of Law in Non-Western Societies', Nader (ed.), *Law in Culture and Society*, p. 18.

a particular outcome is likely to have. The ruler acting as an adjudicator, on the other hand, may well know nothing of the individuals who are in dispute and little of the community in which they live. The 'slice' of the dispute which he can comprehend is, therefore, much smaller than that of a local peace-maker with a closer view. One of the implications of such a restricted view may be that it will often seem easier to fall back on a rule-based decision.

Another implication of state organization, with its line of intermediaries between the ruler and the individual, may be that dispute settlement agencies are organized in a hierarchical fashion. At the apex will be the ruler himself, or some representative he has appointed to deal with disputes; but the path of a disputant to this agency may lead up several links of the chain if, as is typically the case, the ruler's local executives are empowered to deal with disputes. Such an arrangement may well mean that different modes of settlement are applicable at different levels in the hierarchy. The ruler may have empowered his local representatives to dispose of disputes by decision, and to enforce these decisions; but before a dispute comes before a representative, it may be obligatory for efforts to be made to resolve the dispute by the kin of those involved. At this level, the procedure may be mediatory only. We shall consider an example of such a situation later in the chapter. In stateless societies we have already noted that a disputant may have a *choice* of different agencies before which he can take his grievance, but there is no flavour of an 'appellate' structure such as exists in our court system. This element is introduced once you have a hierarchy of agencies; as is the additional complexity inherent in the fact that different modes of settlement may be applicable at different levels in the hierarchy.

Another characteristic of the maintenance of order in a state system, related to the fact that the ruler will have military and police forces at his disposal, is that certain types of conduct may take on a 'public' aspect. Typically, in stateless societies a wrong is only dealt with if some individual feels aggrieved and chooses to take it up through the socially approved means of redress. In a state system, however, there may be some forms of conduct of which the ruler disapproves so strongly that he is prepared to deal with them whether an individual member of the society claims to have been wronged or not. In our own society this public aspect is acknowledged in the distinction drawn between 'civil' and 'criminal' law, and in the corresponding difference between orders as to compensation and fines. While something of this public aspect is probably present in all states, we should not assume that our distinction between civil and criminal matters is necessarily exactly duplicated in other societies.

We also tend to associate our form of state organization with a fairly clear 'separation of powers'; between the legislature, the executive and the judiciary. While some notion of separation of powers may be present in the states we are dealing with, this seldom matches our own system exactly, and very often no such idea is present at all. It may be that the same people carry out the ruler's orders, help him to make the decisions in matters of government, and hear disputes on his behalf. They may also do all these things in the same place, on the same kind of occasion, and the meetings to do with these different functions may not be clearly distinguished.

These features of the state form of organization become much clearer when examples are considered. The example taken here will be the Kgatla,[5] one of a group of Tswana chiefdoms that can be found in present-day Botswana. This society has been chosen partly because I can speak of it at first hand, and partly for two other reasons. The first of these is that the Kgatla state organization has a rare simplicity, being imposed directly upon, and operating through, a system of agnatic descent and an age-set organization (two forms of groupings with which we are familiar from previous chapters). In a slightly simplified form the state can be seen as one giant patrilineage, of which the ruler for the time being is ideally the genealogically senior

5. See generally, Schapera, *A Handbook of Tswana Law and Custom*; *Married Life in an African Tribe*.

male member of the most senior branch; and one of the main channels through which he rules is provided by the senior men at each level in the agnatic system. The other reason for looking at the Kgatla is that in common with other Tswana societies the making of rules through legislation is a well-entrenched practice with them.[6]

The Kgatla occupy a territory of what is today about 2,800 square miles of South East Botswana. There are probably about 35,000 of them, and of these about 20,000 have a permanent home in the ruler's capital, Mochudi; the remainder live in the smaller villages outside or in isolated hamlets in the fields. Although the Kgatla live in a relatively well-watered part of Botswana when one remembers that a large part of the country is made up of the Kalahari desert, by most standards the terrain is very dry. But in most years there is good grazing for cattle, and in perhaps one in three when rain falls in sufficient quantities at the right time, good crops of maize and sorghum may be grown. The Kgatla would certainly see themselves as cattle-keepers first and arable farmers second.

The Kgatla state is governed by an hereditary ruler (*kgosi*),[7] who may turn to three different groupings for advice and help in decision-making. First he is surrounded by a small informal council drawn by him from among his immediate senior relations (his father's and his own younger brothers, his male cousins, his maternal uncles), together with any other men who enjoy special positions of influence and trust. Secondly, he may call together all the headmen of the wards (the name conventionally given to the major administrative divisions into which the society is divided up). Finally, there may be a meeting to which all the adult male members of the society are summoned. Most everyday decisions are taken within the first of these

6. See Schapera, *Tribal Legislation among the Tswana of the Bechuanaland Protectorate*.

7. The state of affairs described here is that which existed in the last years of the nineteenth century, before the Kgatla state was absorbed in the Bechuanaland Protectorate. The Setswana term *kgosi* has conventionally been translated as 'chief', a usage which will be followed here.

groupings and any decision that is reached is then transmitted to the headman of each ward, who himself passes it on down the administrative hierarchy. If more serious matters have to be discussed, all the headmen are summoned; and in matters of the greatest importance all the adult males of the society may be assembled.

The procedure in a meeting at any one of these levels is very flexible, and the actual location of authority is hard to pin down. Typically, the chief raises a matter which he wishes to take action on and speaks about it for a while. Then other people present give their views. Often when a clear view emerges quickly, the chief will summarize it and propose action along that line; there will be choresed assent, and the matter is concluded. The Kgatla would say, though, that it is for the chief to decide; and not for the people at the meeting, whatever level this may be at. In one sense this may be true, but no chief would last long unless he enjoyed general acceptance and this would be swiftly eroded if he constantly tried to push through measures for which there was no support.

Many of the major decisions which are taken in these councils require action by large groups if they are to be carried out: in the past, if war was to be made, or the state organized for defence; today, if the cattle are to be rounded up, or if major water-works are to be dug. Where anything like this has to be done, the age-sets will be called to do it. A new age-set is formed every five years or so when the young males of the society then approaching physical manhood are gathered together and submitted to initiation procedures (including circumcision). All those initiated together form the new set; and as the new sets are successively formed over the years, those above rise in seniority. The physically hardest work, such as major building projects and (formerly) making war, is left to the members of the more junior sets.

The link between the chief and the senior man in each ward is ideally a genealogical one, for the office of chief should devolve from father to eldest son, while the younger sons of each ruler go off to form their own wards, assuming administrative control of these new sub-divisions of the main group. The Kgatla believe that their society was founded by Kgafela in the late seventeenth or early eighteenth century, and most of the forty-eight wards in the central village of Mochudi today are headed by men claiming descent from younger brothers of chiefs descended from Kgafela. A few wards whose members do not claim descent from younger brothers of former chiefs have been founded by men of groupings previously conquered by the Kgatla, or who have asked for permission to join them for defence against a common enemy. But apart from these exceptions, ward heads are senior members of junior branches of the chief's agnatic group.

This system of administration is reflected at ground level in the residential organization of the main village. At the centre is a group of homesteads occupied by men of the chief's immediate agnatic segment, and ranged around this are forty-seven other groups of homesteads, each presided over by a ward head. Thus, the ward in this sense constitutes a geographical area; and each headman ideally lives with those over whom he has administrative control and responsibility.

Within each ward there may be anything from 200 to 600 people, and the majority of the members again claim to be related in the male line to the headman. Two further sub-divisions are also generally found inside a ward. First, all the males claiming descent from a common grandfather tend to be grouped together, and within such a sub-group a minimal unit is made up of an adult married male, occupying a homestead with his wife (or wives) and children. In many wards also, there have been incorporated individuals from other tribes who have come over time to form their own descent groups under the administrative control of the headman who is a member of the major segment.

Thus, if the group is looked at from the bottom up there is first the married male heading his own household, then the group consisting of his closest male agnates, then an aggregate of such groups forming a ward, and lastly the wards together forming the total society. Kgatla society can thus be seen as an ever-growing and deepening pyramid, the base of which is extended as more males are born and rear their own families; while in its simplest form the political and administrative organization is imposed on the agnatic system like a cloak.

The Kgatla see the regularities of their everyday lives as governed by a corpus of rules which they describe as *mekgwa le melao ya Sekgatla*, a phrase which has generally been translated as 'Kgatla law and custom'. However, this translation is misleading in two ways. First, the terms *melao* and *mekgwa* are not sharply distinguished in the way that this translation would suggest. Secondly, 'Kgatla law and custom' cannot be seen as a body of rules corresponding directly to our rules of law, because the term embraces a whole repertoire of norms of different kinds, ranging from rules of polite behaviour and etiquette, through moral imperatives and rules taken very seriously in the context of dispute, and even includes examples of what we would call legislation. Everyone, even the chief, is expected to comply with these rules in their everyday behaviour, and there is a Tswana saying: *'Molao sefofu, obile otle oje mong waone'* – 'The law is blind, it eats even its owner.' But there is not the distinct category of 'legal' rules which so clearly characterizes our system. Norms governing social behaviour on a visit to someone else's homestead fall just as clearly within the overall classification as those prescribing what must be done when one man's cattle destroy another man's field of corn.

The origin of some of these rules is seen by the Kgatla to lie in long-established and adhered-to patterns of approved behaviour, others as arising out of decisions made by a chief in handling a dispute, yet others out of direct announcements made by him in what we would see as statutory form. The Kgatla would distinguish among such announcements those which simply restate and emphasize something which already forms part of 'Kgatla law and custom', but which has perhaps become forgotten or carelessly observed. The occasion of any meeting in the chief's *kgotla* may provide an opportunity for such a reminder. On the other hand, an announcement which either expressly changes some existing rule, or which provides a new regulation to deal with some special contingency, has to be introduced with more careful preparation. The Kgatla say that when a chief wishes to make a change of this kind he should call together the tribesmen so that the matter can be discussed. Only when he has done this, and following discussion in the *kgotla* announces a new rule, does such a rule become part of 'Kgatla law and custom'.

Although the Kgatla would say that it is for the ruler to announce a new law, most would agree that he *should not* do so unless the proposal he has already put to the *kgotla* meeting meets with approval. Where such a proposal does not attract support few would say that this prohibits a ruler from going ahead with his announcement, for there is a saying to the effect that 'The chief's word is law' ('*Lentswe lakgosi kemolao*'), but the chances of such a rule being generally complied with are greatly lessened.

Rules which Kgatla and other Tswana chiefs have announced in this way extend over a very broad field of subjects, including family life (e.g. how many wives a man may marry; what he must give by way of bridewealth; the age of a woman at marriage; the number of cattle payable as compensation when one man impregnates someone else's daughter); land tenure (regulations relating to the fencing of fields and the settling of uncleared land); public hygiene; and traffic regulations (e.g. to the effect that wagons must be fitted with proper brakes for going downhill).[8]

The extent to which one of these legislative announcements gets complied with depends upon the degree of social acceptance which it achieves and upon the capacity of the chief to enforce it. Some chiefs do not announce a measure until they feel that it will enjoy widespread acceptance, and in such a case enforcement presents few difficulties. Where a rule does

8. See Schapera, *Tribal Legislation among the Tswana of the Bechuanaland Protectorate*.

not enjoy social approval, or where it is burdensome to comply with, much depends on the energy of the chief. If it involves such a matter as the fencing of the fields or the branding of stock, the matter can be handled through rigorous inspections and the punishment of those who fail to comply. On the other hand, chiefs who have tried to regulate family life have found this much harder to achieve.

As well as providing signposts for proper social behaviour, *mekgwa le melao ya Sekgatla* are also seen as furnishing the criteria according to which disputes should be settled where these arise. All Kgatla talk freely about these rules, and consider that they know them; there is no sense in which they are the special preserve of some particular sub-group within the society. In the context of a dispute these rules may be expressly invoked, or more frequently referred to by implication through the way in which the details of a particular claim are presented. People are taken to know the rules, and the mere claim that 'Molefe's son has impregnated my daughter' or 'Lesoka's cattle have trampled my corn' is sufficient to invoke by implication the body of rules which everyone knows to be associated with impregnation of unmarried women and the damage to crops by cattle. As in most societies, *mekgwa le melao* differ considerably in their degree of generality, and it is possible for them to be adduced in the context of a dispute in such a way as to conflict. Where, for example, two brothers are in dispute over who should inherit the mother's homestead, the one may invoke a general rule to the effect that close agnates should live peacefully together, whereas the other may rely on the much more detailed prescription to the effect that the youngest son should inherit the dwelling. It is where conflicting rules are relied on like this that it becomes necessary to talk about rules explicitly. Where both disputants agree as to the rules, but argue about the interpretation of facts in relation to an agreed rule, explicit reference is unnecessary.[9]

9. See Comaroff and Roberts, 'The Invocation of Norms in Dispute Settlement: The Tswana Case', Hamnett (ed.), *Social Anthropology and Law*.

Settlement-directed discussion is seen under all circumstances as the most appropriate way to handle a dispute. While retaliatory violence and forceable re-taking of property are tolerated within narrow limits, these never enjoy social approval. Similarly, while it is recognized that supernatural agencies may be invoked in order to establish responsibility for harm or misfortune that has been suffered, further resort to these agencies when a human is identified as responsible is strongly discouraged. Such methods are recognized as likely to exacerbate a dispute in the event of their discovery by the other party.

The agencies for handling a dispute are located in the institutional hierarchy we have already considered. Where a quarrel breaks out between two people, the Kgatla see it as their own responsibility to try and settle it between themselves through bilateral discussion; but because they realize that such negotiations may fail, and that the help of third parties may be necessary, they each keep their senior kinsmen in touch with what is going on from a very early stage. Relatively simple and recurring problems, like the destruction of crops by cattle, are typically resolved at this level; but where the matter is more serious, or where there has been a history of bad relations between the parties, the trouble may be taken directly to senior kinsmen. Under such circumstances, with tempers running high, attempts at bilateral negotiation may be avoided entirely through fear that a fight will break out.

Where bilateral attempts at settlement fail, or where they are not made through fear that they will lead to violence and a heightening of the trouble, the disputants call on their immediate kin to resolve the matter. Although the Kgatla rely heavily on their close agnates for help in disputes, trouble is seldom contained as closely within this group as we saw it to be in the case of the Arusha, and close maternal kinsmen are likely to be drawn in from the beginning. These approaches may culminate in private negotiations or a formal meeting at the homestead of a senior member of the group to which either disputant belongs. The mode of settlement attempted at this level depends upon the relationship of the parties. Where they are not close kinsmen, the respective disputants typically meet with their kin in support, and then the two groups try to feel their way towards a settlement by negotiation, without anyone seeking to mediate from a bridging position. Where they are related, a senior kinsman who can claim equally close relationship to both may try to mediate from a neutral standpoint. At this level no-one is in a position to impose a decision, and if a compromise cannot be reached through negotiation, the matter has to be taken to the headman within whose ward the earlier meetings have been held.

The headman has a range of options available to him in dealing with the dispute. He may attempt to mediate directly by suggesting solutions which may possibly be acceptable to both parties; or he may send them away for further discussion with their close kinsmen if he feels that the possibilities of that avenue have not been exhausted. However, although the headman may act as a mediator if he wishes, it is also recognized that he may attempt to resolve the matter by imposing a decision. Where he does so, the parties have the choice of accepting and complying with his decision, or taking the dispute to the chief. Where the matter is taken to the chief, he hears the report of the headman who dealt with the dispute earlier and the accounts of the disputants and their respective senior kinsmen. Then, like the headman, he may attempt to mediate, or proceed directly to resolve the matter by decision. Once a decision has been given, the chief has the capacity to enforce it if necessary. Disobedience will be met with corporal punishment, the confiscation of stock or the withdrawal of land allocations. The age-set organization provides the necessary machinery for enforcement: members of one of the more junior sets can be sent out to bring a recalcitrant individual before the chief or collect together his stock prior to confiscation.

Thus in this Kgatla example settlement-directed talk enjoys pre-eminence as a mode of handling disputes, while such means as violent self-help and sorcery are strongly disapproved. In the settlement of disputes, as in the ordering of everyday life,

people are expected to follow *mekgwa le melao*; but this repertoire of norms, ranging from the general to the particular,
offers the Kgatla considerable flexibility in managing their lives
and in dealing with disputes. Nor can it be accurately seen
as a discrete corpus of legal rules, ranging as it does from
norms of polite behaviour to mandatory statutory injunctions.
Further, it does not constitute a monolithic system, as variations in content and in interpretation can be found both in
different geographical areas and at different levels in the state
organization.

The hierarchical organization of the Kgatla state is also
matched in the organization of agencies of dispute settlement, as
attempts at resolution should move from the disputants themselves, to the descent group, to the ward, and finally to the
chief. Further, while negotiatory and mediatory means of
settlement may be attempted at all levels, these give way in the
last resort to a judicial mode before a headman or the chief,
while the latter has access to organized force in ensuring compliance with any decision if this should prove to be necessary.

The Kgatla state represents a single example in which all the
crucial features of centralized political organization are clearly
present, and which exhibits the kind of control institutions to
be expected under those arrangements. Other examples might
have been given which would have differed in detail from the
Kgatla case. In particular, the exact organizational features
upon which the state is superimposed and through which the
ruler exercises his power may vary considerably; the very simplicity of the Kgatla example, with the state fitted so neatly
to an agnatic system, may even be unusual. Similarly, the
ruler may often claim a rather closer association with the
supernatural than does the Kgatla chief. Although he is seen
as an intermediary between his people and supernatural agents,
and as such is believed to play an essential part in summon-
ing rain, he does not (unlike some other African kings) claim
divine ancestry. Nonetheless, the example does convey the
essence of the state system, if that is taken to 'consist in the

delegation of power by the ruler who holds final authority, in such a way that he can expect his orders or decisions to be carried out throughout the land which he claims to rule'.[10]

10. Mair, *Primitive Government*, p. 138.

9
Fighting and Talking

Reflecting on the different ways in which trouble may be handled, Bohannan has suggested that there are 'basically two forms of conflict resolution: administered rules and fighting. Law and war.'[1] This stark observation is certainly thought-provoking, but the ethnographic examples we examined in Chapters 5 to 8 indicate that Bohannan's formulation is too terse. First, it is clear that under certain conditions disputes can be resolved without fighting, through bilateral discussion or mediatory procedures, even where rules are not clear-cut and are not seen by the actors to be of paramount importance. Secondly, as the Maring case so strikingly illustrates, where fighting does take place its form may be closely regulated by socially approved rules. Nonetheless, Bohannan does force us to consider the fact that there seems to be much more fighting in some societies than in others; and that societies appear to vary in the importance which members attach to rules. In this and the following chapter we pursue these problems further, drawing together the material we have already examined to see what may be concluded about the conditions under which different means of resolving disputes are likely to be found.

From the examples that we are familiar with it seems that we are faced with two apparent polarities. First is the opposition between fighting and talking: the fact that inter-personal violence is more prominent as a means of resolving conflict in some societies and talking in others. Secondly there is the relationship between rules and power: the fact that rules seem to play a central part in some settlement processes whereas

1. The Introduction to *Law and Warfare*, p. xiii.

pragmatic considerations, and the exercise of power, seem more important in others. Bohannan's formulation runs these polarities together so as to imply that the alternative of fighting or talking, and of resolving disputes in accordance with the balance of power rather than the application of rules, represent no more than two sides of the same coin. Certainly they are closely related; but for the present purposes it seems best to separate consideration of the procedures whereby disputes are resolved (fighting and talking) from the analytically distinct question of the criteria which govern these processes (rules and power). Some overlap is inevitable, but we consider the fighting/talking dichotomy primarily in this chapter, and return to the relationship of rules and power in Chapter 10.

A classification which attempts no more than to divide societies into those where quarrels are resolved through fighting and those where they are handled through talking must be too crude. We have already recognized that in *any* society a number of control mechanisms are likely to exist side by side and together contribute to the prevention and handling of disputes. The Nuer example also shows that fighting and talking may coexist, even if their relative importance differs markedly from one society to another. Furthermore, the scale of inter-personal violence ensuing upon a quarrel is infinitely varied. It may be limited to private acts of retaliatory violence inflicted upon a wrongdoer by his victim; it may involve protracted fighting between two segments of the same ethnic group, or warfare between groups of different ethnic affiliations. Similarly, the form of the encounter may range from a limited and highly formalized exchange of blows to uncontrolled fighting. The conceivable kinds of occasions of settlement-directed talk are just as numerous.

It is also important to be clear at this stage as to the nature of the question we are asking. We are not concerned here with why quarrels arise in human societies, or what people in different groups ostensibly quarrel about, but with why quarrels are predominantly handled one way here and differently somewhere else. Certainly there may be a relationship between the nature and source of a particular dispute and the manner in which it is handled, but our primary concern is with gross differences in approach to trouble observable from one society to another.

One difficulty we are faced with in asking this kind of question must also be kept in mind at this point. For reasons related to the historical development of colonial expansion and to the growth of social anthropology as a discipline, small-scale societies have been studied in very different stages of 'contact' with external, particularly western, influences. Whereas some had been subject to colonial rule for generations before being seriously studied by anthropologists, in others the anthropologist arrived before or more or less at the same time as the trader and administrator. While these differences do not explain the variations we are concerned with, they need to be taken into account in assessing them.

Leaving that reservation on one side, few easy or entirely satisfactory explanations of why there is more fighting in some societies than others have been arrived at. But we can clarify the issues involved and indicate directions which a search for the answers might take. In attempting to explain the differential resort to fighting it is possible to phrase the problem in two ways, not necessarily inconsistent with each other, but involving different points of departure. One approach is to isolate those conditions which are felt likely to cause fighting, leaving the question of talking very much on one side. The other approach is founded on the assumption that fighting will arise where conditions are unfavourable for talking, and thus begins by trying to establish what these latter conditions are. The end result of these enquiries is often similar, but the paths taken are instructive and it is worth following each of them here.

A. FIGHTING

In looking for explanations of why there is more fighting in some societies than in others, two tentative generalizations may be suggested. First, perhaps predictably, there seems to be a close link between approved values and the actual incidence of inter-personal violence. It is typically in those societies where postures of independent, aggressive self-reliance are encouraged that disputes most often end in violent confrontation. Secondly, although the nature of the link is unclear, it seems that in those societies where private retaliatory violence is common inter-group fighting is also most frequently observed. In such societies a typical syndrome involves the escalation of violent retaliation for a wrong into fighting between groups to which the original disputants belong. This is seen notably in some New Guinea societies where sporadic fighting between adjacent communities of the same ethnic group is found in conjunction with a high level of inter-personal violence within the group.

Some of the most widely advanced explanations of the differential resort to fighting link the prevalence of violence to particular forms of social and political organization. These theories vary considerably both in terms of the structural features identified and in the nature of the explanation put forward. Much also depends upon an underlying assumption: Is it the fighting or the absence of it which has to be explained? Do we look for structural features which may contribute towards the containment of quarrels or those which might exacerbate them?

One prominent theory holds that disputes lead to fighting only where the organizational arrangements are not conducive to coercive intervention by third parties. The clearest conditions under which such intervention is likely to be found are those where there is some kind of state organization under which the ruler has police or military agencies at his disposal. Outside such a society, third parties capable of intervening forcibly to prevent fighting (or willing to do so) will not necessarily be found. In support of this view we can certainly note that most rulers disapprove strongly of sustained fighting among their subjects, encourage the use of dispute-settlement procedures which do not involve inter-personal violence, and do their best to terminate (by force if need be) any fights which do break out.

Given that extensive fighting is seldom tolerated in established states, we are thus largely concerned with differences between one acephalous society and another. In some of these societies followings tend to form round ephemeral leaders who, by virtue of individual ascendancy, are able to coerce any adherents who fight among themselves; but action of this kind may be sporadic and fail to represent a consistently present control mechanism. Moreover, 'big men' may not be interested in controlling disputes among those they live with, or acquire prestige from doing so. There are reports of the members of small face-to-face communities getting together to drive out or kill wrongdoers whose activities threaten the security of the group as a whole;[2] but such accounts seem relatively rare. Generally, it seems that only with the growth of a state organization does wrongdoing acquire a 'public' aspect which leads those not immediately involved to undertake coercive intervention.

The weakness of any theory which attributes fighting to the absence of third parties capable of undertaking coercive action is emphasized by the existence of numerous relatively peaceful societies in which such third parties are absent. The Ndendeuli provide an example we are familiar with. More persuasive are those arguments which postulate the need for some kind of third-party intervention if disputes are to be peacefully resolved, but which do not require such intervention to be coercive. Koch puts forward such a theory in attempting to account for the high level of inter-personal violence in Jale society. In his view, the prevalence of fighting there is due to the fact that 'very ineffective methods exist to transform a dyadic confrontation into a triadic relationship which could secure a settlement by the intervention of the third party'.[3] We consider the conditions under which intervention by third

2. For example the Kamba institution known as *kingolle*: see Middleton, *The Kikuyu and Kamba of Kenya*.
3. *War and Peace in Jalemo*, p. 159.

parties as mediators is feasible in the next section of this chapter, and it is sufficient for the moment to point out that some circumstances are unfavourable to such intervention. These may exist, for example, in a society composed of agnatic groupings where men belonging to two different lineages become involved in a quarrel. Support on both sides may be readily forthcoming, but there may be no-one from a larger aggregation in the society capable of mediating. In this situation, the dispute may well escalate into fighting between the two groups concerned.

Here we should note that some theorists go even further than suggesting that in societies made up of localized agnatic segments fighting may take place because there are no third parties capable of intervening. They argue that in certain types of residential grouping, notably those based on a core of patrilineal kinsmen, power groups are likely to develop, the members of which will be prepared to promote their common interests, by force if necessary, against other communities. Where these discrete power groups form, a wrong against one member may be seen as a wrong against the group, with the result that whole communities are readily drawn into conflict with each other: 'in societies with power groups every act of violence elicits a chain reaction and there is danger of any individual deed of aggression leading to group conflict'.[4] Cross-cultural surveys which show a correlation between patrilocal residence and fighting among segments of common origin offer some support for this theory.[5] The theory certainly seems consistent with the readiness to fight which characterizes the relations of groupings made up of patrilineal kinsmen encountered in societies like the Jale and Maring.

4. Van Velzen and van Wetering, 'Residence, Power Groups and Intra-Societal Aggression: An Enquiry into the Conditions Leading to Peacefulness in Non-Stratified Societies', *Int. Arch. Ethnog.*, vol. 49, 169–200.

5. See, for example, Otterbein, 'Internal War: A Cross-cultural Study', *American Anthropologist*, vol. 70, 227–89; Divale, Chamberis, Gangloff, 'War, Peace and Marital Residence in Pre-Industrial Societies', *Journal of Conflict Resolution*, vol. 20, 57–78.

But it does not explain the high level of violence which is apparently also found *within* some of these communities, where it might have been anticipated that shared interests and common enemies would have encouraged the peaceful solution of internal difficulties.

Theorists seeking to identify structural features which may *discourage* fighting between communities have focused on cross-cutting affiliations of the kind which Colson identified as being of central importance in the control of conflict in the case of the Plateau Tonga.[6] As we have already seen, it is argued that the cleavage of loyalty to which such conflicting ties give rise may militate against disputes enduring over time and prevent them broadening in scope in such a way as to embattle consistently opposed groups within the society. The absence of such ties has been invoked to explain the continuing violence which characterizes the relations of some New Guinea communities;[7] but here again the lack of these ties between neighbouring groups does not help to explain the incidence of violent quarrels *within* them.

In the context of these theories which hold that fighting between groups with shared ethnic affiliations may be linked with particular forms of political and social organization, we should also consider the widespread view that conflict between groups leads to heightened cohesion within them. This theory can be traced back at least as far as Sumner and Simmel. The former expressed it as follows: 'The relation of comradeship and peace in the we-group and that of hostility and war towards other-groups are correlative to each other. The exigencies of war with outsiders are what make peace inside.'[8] Several modern anthropologists have put forward examples in support of this idea, and some have gone further to argue that it is the need to maintain internal cohesion that leads to fighting with other groups.[9] The theory may well hold under some circum-

6. See Chapter 4, p. 56 above.
7. For example Koch, *War and Peace in Jalemo*, pp. 166 *et seq.*
8. *Folkways*, p. 12.
9. For instance Murphy, 'Intergroup Hostility and Social Cohesion', *American Anthropologist*, vol. 59, 1018–35, p. 1032.

stances, but it does seem that in the case of a number of societies, including the Jale, fighting between groups goes side by side with a good deal of violence within the group as well.

Some other widely advanced explanations of the differential resort to fighting centre around the occurrence of particular ecological conditions. One such theory argues that fighting between groups may be explained by population growth leading to shortages of land. In this connection quite a number of studies do show that in societies where land disputes are frequent these disputes end in fighting, and that the winners sometimes take over the fields or gardens of the losers. The explanation is convincing up to a point, but certain reservations must be noted which can be illustrated if we turn back to the Maring example. There Rappaport puts forward the view tentatively that inter-group fighting may be started by land shortage, even though a majority of battles seem, immediately at least, attributable to other kinds of dispute. His data further indicate that only a minority of fights lead to the rout of one side by the other, and that even where one side is driven away the other rarely takes over their arable lands. It may also be said that explanations of this kind seem to beg a vital question: Why do these quarrels lead to *fighting*? Even if we accept that in these societies there are many quarrels about land, and that these are due to its shortage, this does not in itself explain the fighting. There are other acephalous societies in which land is short and disputes over it are endemic but where quarrels are resolved by other means. Rappaport's theory seems particularly vulnerable to this objection. He specifically links tension with fighting and suggests that if you find the major 'sources of irritation' in a society, you identify the causes of the fighting.[10] If we were concerned simply with why there should be a particular kind of dispute repeatedly arising in a given society his explanation would be satisfactory, but we are considering the further question of why some kinds of disputes lead to fighting. This latter problem cannot be dealt with merely by identifying important sources of tension which repeatedly lead to quarrels.

10. *Pigs for the Ancestors: Ritual in the Ecology of a New Guinea People*, p. 116.

Recurring sources of trouble can be found in any group; the difficulty is why these are handled in some cases through fighting, but not in others.

B. TALKING

An alternative way of explaining the differential resort to fighting as a means of resolving trouble lies through an examination of the conditions favourable to settlement-directed talking. Here the argument runs as follows: 'Where procedures for resolving disputes through settlement-directed talking are well established, fighting is unlikely to be resorted to. Hence, if we can find out the conditions favourable and unfavourable to the various forms of settlement-directed talk, we also arrive at an understanding of those conditions under which fighting is likely to occur.' At first sight this approach does not appear particularly promising as it rests on the uncertain assumption that talking and fighting are true alternatives, and that people will talk rather than fight if they get the chance. But it is fair to assume that it will provide some help because the available evidence does seem to suggest that it is in those societies where talking is least well established as a means of handling disputes that fighting is most prevalent.

In much of the literature it is taken for granted that the peaceful resolution of quarrels by talking depends on the presence of third parties, and that attempts at such settlement will necessarily fail where there are no effective arrangements for third-party intervention. We have already seen how Koch sadly attributes the prevalence of fighting in Jale society to the absence of effective procedures for third-party intervention.[11] In my view this assumption is mistaken, and under certain conditions bilateral processes can be perfectly feasible; but there is no doubt that effective third-party intervention is a very important element of many settlement processes. The circumstances under which it is possible must therefore be considered before we turn to those conducive to bilateral procedures.

In Chapter 4 we isolated two basic forms which settlement-

11. See p. 158 above.

directed talk initiated through the intervention of a third party might take: mediatory processes and those involving third-party decision. The latter mode of settlement may only take place where some umpire is in a position to force his adjudication upon the parties, or where they volunteer to bring the dispute before him for decision. The former conditions are most likely to be found in the centralized state, where the ruler himself adjudicates, or empowers his executives to do this for him. In either case both the intervention itself and any decision which is made may be enforced through state agencies. Outside such a society, leaders may sometimes be in a position to enforce their decisions on members of a following but will seldom be able to do so with much consistency and regularity. Apart from these cases where the third party is in a position to impose his presence on the disputants, the introduction of an umpire presents much greater difficulties. Not only must third-party decision be an approved mode of settlement, but, further, an undoubted neutral must be found to perform this role. This requirement of neutrality assumes even greater importance in processes of arbitration than it does in mediatory processes, as in the latter the parties themselves retain ultimate control over the outcome.

In many acephalous societies the possibility of submitting a dispute to a third party for decision is inconceivable. For the Nuer male, for example, such a submission would imply weakness amounting to a denial of manhood. In other cases, as we saw in the Arusha example, organizational forms *within* the group may militate against neutrality, while to look outside conflicts with notions of privacy. Furthermore, the idea that a truly neutral person could be persuaded to look at someone else's dispute seriously is apparently laughable to the Arusha.

In the few instances of third-party decision reported from acephalous societies, the arbitrator seems invariably to be a figure standing somewhat 'outside' the system. This is certainly the case with the saintly figures who are called upon to arbitrate in disputes among the Swat Pathans.[12] A similar role appears

12. Barth, *Political Leadership among the Swat Pathans*.

to be performed by religious specialists in Berber[13] and Somali[14] communities. These three cases suggest that a marginal situation must be supplemented by other attributes, such as a state of grace or privileged access to supernatural agencies, before a person may arbitrate successfully in an acephalous group.

In any society the conditions favourable to a mediated settlement must be difficult to achieve in that not only must third parties with suitable attributes be prepared to intervene but the disputants themselves must be disposed to a settlement. As we noted in Chapter 4, a mediator must be ostensibly impartial and thus not too closely identified with either side in terms of such things as kinship and economic cooperation. As an individual he must also possess further attributes which make him acceptable. These seem to vary from one society to another but may consist of proven skill, advanced age, genealogical seniority or special piety. Some writers have insisted that mediators must necessarily stand 'outside the system' if they are to be successful. One has said that 'so much attention has been devoted by sociologists to [the identity and qualifications of mediators] that it is now generally accepted that mediators are always, regardless of the level of civilization or technology, chosen from among those individuals who by virtue of their professional, political, kinship, or ideological status stand somewhat outside the system'.[15] While it is clear that in some societies mediatory functions are carried out by those who occupy marginal positions, this characteristic is by no means universal. In the Ndendeuli case, while successful mediation is certainly a source of prestige, and ambitious men are therefore eager to adopt this role, the central qualification seems to be equidistant from the disputants in terms of kinship and cooperation.[16]

13. Gellner, *Saints of the Atlas.*

14. Lewis, *A Pastoral Democracy.*

15. Black-Michaud, *Cohesive Force: Feud in the Mediterranean and the Middle East*, p. 93.

16. 'Dispute Settlement without Courts: The Ndendeuli of Southern Tanzania', Nader (ed.), *Law in Culture and Society*, pp. 32–3.

Similar attributes are looked for in the mediators who operate at the lower levels of the Kgatla dispute-settlement processes, and my own experience of those procedures was that aspiring politicians and religio-medical experts were seldom seen as reliable mediators. It would certainly be a mistake to suggest that mediators *need* necessarily be 'marginal' in any other sense than that implied by avoidance of close identification with either party. In a number of studies which emphasize the marginal character of successful interveners no very clear distinction is drawn between mediators and arbitrators.[17] The available ethnographic accounts suggest that arbitrators rather than mediators require to possess this attribute.[18]

While mediatory processes of dispute settlement are widely reported in stateless societies, the requirement of neutrality is often made hard to satisfy by the organizational forms which some of these societies take. For example, in a dispute involving two neighbouring communities a successful mediator must come from outside either group, and for that reason may be hard to find; there may simply be no higher-level grouping in the society out of which he can emerge. The Maring communities which Rappaport describes provide just such a case.[19] The requirement of impartiality can present similar difficulties in small, unstratified communities where it may be impossible to find third parties who are not too closely aligned (in terms of kinship or economic cooperation) with one or other of the disputants. In some instances the organization of groupings within the society is such that no-one in the group could be seen as occupying a neutral position by both parties; thus we saw in the Arusha case how lineages are sub-divided in such a way that any member knows exactly where his allegiance lies in the event of trouble, leaving no room for members to play a mediatory role. Furthermore, where a mediator can only be found outside the group there may be other reasons why such an outsider would be unacceptable. In the Arusha case a notion

17. See, for instance, Black-Michaud, op. cit., p. 11, note 2.
18. See p. 163 above.
19. See pp. 117–20 above.

that lineage matters are private to the group inhibits the choice of neutral mediators from other segments.

Despite the importance widely attached to third-party intervention in dispute-settlement processes, conditions conducive to bilateral negotiations are at first sight the simplest to achieve. All that is required is that the parties themselves, and any supporters lined up behind them, should be disposed towards reaching a settlement by this means. Further, as we saw in the Arusha example,[20] this mode of handling disputes is in practice perfectly viable where talking, and a disposition to compromise, constitute approved responses to trouble in the society concerned. The method also obviates the need to secure the help of neutral third parties – a form of assistance which is certainly problematic under some conditions. Nothwithstanding such advantages, the necessary conditions for bilateral negotiation are in other ways difficult to achieve. Particularly where the quarrel arises out of some serious wrong such as a killing, or the seizure of a highly valued item of property, the initial contact may be hard to establish without the risk of escalating violence, and the ensuing dialogue similarly difficult to maintain. Even if all this is successfully achieved, and an acceptable agreement reached, the parties may well find it hard to keep this agreement in the absence of third-party assistance.

These latter difficulties suggest that the limitations upon the use of this method of settlement are as much related to the values prevailing in a given society as to particular features of social organization. To be successful, bilateral negotiation must be seen as the 'right' way of resolving a dispute: the ready disposition to talk and the conciliatory gesture must represent approved responses. Where honour demands retaliation to an assumed wrong and where conciliatory approaches are likely to be identified as signs of weakness, bilateral negotiation can have little chance of success; and if talking is to be established the need for some third party in a bridging position (if only as a go-between) becomes acute. We need only compare societies like the Nuer and Arusha to see how closely this method of

20. See pp. 128–34.

settlement depends for success on the configuration of values in the group concerned.

In seeking to answer questions of the kind posed in this chapter we have to be particularly careful not to let the arguments be coloured by our own values and preconceptions. Most people in our society would probably subscribe to the assumption that peaceful solutions to disputes are 'right' and ultimately sought by almost everybody; where these are not achieved something has gone wrong with the mechanism. Under these circumstances it is difficult to recognize at first sight the loaded nature of any hypothesis which looks at conflict in terms of 'failure' to develop particular forms of settlement, such as those involving judicial intervention. Nonetheless, we must accept that for some peoples fighting represents the proper means of handling a quarrel; for them sitting and talking will not represent the right way, even a conceivable way, of reaching a solution. Why this should be so is not something which can be fully explained by turning to particular ecological conditions or socio-political formations. The limited scope of such explanations is plain from the cases we have considered. Even if we accept, to take the Jale example, that political conditions do not favour third-party intervention, bilateral processes could be followed were talking seen as an approved mode of settlement. Similarly, there are features of Jale society which could be important in restraining conflict were they utilized: the 'big men' who could interest themselves more in dispute settlement if they chose; the links between the members of the men's house group could operate to restrain intra-group violence; the exchange relationships associated with affinal links could inhibit inter-group fighting; and the threat of attack from 'other districts' could also draw together neighbouring communities. But the possibilities presented by these avenues are not fully exhausted; it does not accord with Jale values to do so.

10
Rules and Power

The opposition which Bohannan postulates between 'administered rules' and 'fighting' also implies that compliance with
rule and the exercise of power represent alternative means of
securing order and settling disputes – a suggestion which takes
us back to fundamental questions about the basis of order over
which sociological theorists are deeply divided. While some see
compliance with mutually accepted rules as being at the root of
order in any society, others lay much greater stress on the
exercise of power as the means through which societies are held
together. However, the examples which we have been considering suggest that what purport to be rival explanations of social
order in fact rely upon different, but complementary, features
found in all societies. Thus, whatever importance agreement as
to rules may take on, the clashes of interest emphasized by
conflict theorists are also inevitable concomitants of social life;
and however obtrusive the exercise of power or the pursuit of
interests may seem these must take place in any society within
the context of some normative framework. Consequently, we
would do best to start out by seeing the operation of rules and
the exercise of power as concurrent features, closely inter-
linked, of any social life; it is their exact relationship and the
precise balance struck between them which deserves further
investigation.

Certainly it is possible to set up hypothetical situations under
which rules are dominant, and oppose these to cases in which
differences are resolved in accordance with the distribution of
power. We can imagine, on the one hand, a society in which
rules are clear-cut, reasonably comprehensive, and enjoy widespread acceptance as signposts to proper conduct. Further, it

might be understood in such a society that where quarrels arise they should be resolved in accordance with rules. In the last resort there might be agencies available to adjudicate between disputing parties and impose a rule-based decision. Such a society could be contrasted with conditions under which no rules are explicitly articulated, in which it is understood that each must pursue his interests as best he can, and in which achievement is measured in terms of successful pursuit of those interests. Where disputes arise which are not resolved through physical force, these are handled through bargaining, in accordance with the relative strength of the respective parties. The only limitations placed upon the exercise of either party's muscle are those of a pragmatic character. However, such cases represent models only, which could never be exactly duplicated in practice. We have only to think about some of the societies we have examined to see how far from reality these models are. For example, it is often in those small, unstratified societies composed of kin-based groups – where the element of consensus seems at first sight to hold overriding importance – that life is seen by the participants as entirely a matter of pursuing interests. Similarly, it is sometimes in those larger, hierarchically organized societies with centralized government – where the exercise of power seems to the outsider more obtrusive – that compliance with rule is most explicitly and firmly stressed in the ideology.

In this chapter an attempt is made to elucidate the extent to which the relationship of rules and power may differ from one society to another, and to consider how far variations in this relationship may be linked to differences in societal form and settlement process. In doing so it is necessary to note first some wide variations in the clarity with which rules are perceived and articulated, the way in which they are seen to operate, and the value attached to norm-oriented behaviour.

I have already argued that as a basis for everyday life in any community there must of necessity be some shared assumptions among the members as to how people behave in familiar situations.[1] This must be so even in the very smallest or most loosely knit communities. In the simplest societies these assumptions need only relate to the sharing of food and to sexual access; but in many others they must cover a much wider range to take in such matters as the management of land and cattle, and the control of other scarce and valued resources. In any society some elements of this normative base must be implicit in its fundamental organizational features and visible from the outside to an observer as he watches the repeated patterns of everyday life. Some types of relationship and some courses of conduct will recur over and over again, while others will be generally avoided. Nevertheless, the extent to which such observed regularities are matched by explicitly articulated rules, and the relative importance which is attached to such rules by members of the group, must be treated as variable.

While we tend to think and speak freely about normative propositions, this is not always the case elsewhere. As early researchers found to their surprise, some peoples have difficulty in supplying an inventory of their 'laws and customs', or indeed thinking and talking in normative terms at all. Hoebel, for example, found this to be the case in his work among the Comanche Indians.[2] Not only did they seem unable to quote any abstract norms as being applicable to their social lives, but they were also perplexed when he asked them what the correct behaviour would be in certain hypothetical situations. Elsewhere, on the other hand, people speak fluently in normative terms and readily supply a catalogue of approved rules. Such differences must have profound implications in the conduct of everyday life and for the settlement of disputes.

At the same time we must bear in mind that the comprehension of rules and the importance attached to them is not necessarily related to the degree of explicitness with which they are discussed. In some societies rules are of crucial importance in decision-making and yet few express references are made to

1. See p. 31 above.
2. *The Political Organisation and Law-Ways of the Comanche Indians*, American Anthropological Association, Memoir 54.

them at all. As the anthropologist Fallers has put it, some people 'very seldom talk about the law – about the reach of the concept of wrong. They talk instead about the "facts" – about what happened – without articulating the legal significance of these events.'[3] Where this is the case a claim may be made and the facts on which it is based adduced in such a way that the normative proposition upon which it is founded is implicit. For example, in connection with claims for compensation in respect of damage to crops by cattle among the Tswana I have often heard men detail at great length the nature and extent of damage to standing crops and conclude with a demand for a bag of corn by way of compensation. The respondent then replies by denying that his cattle were in the area, or by asserting that the damage caused was too small to warrant a full sack of corn. Finally, the headman may simply say: 'X, your cattle trampled Y's crops, you must give Y the bag of corn he asks for.' At no stage in the dispute has any rule been explicitly invoked, but argument and decision proceed on the shared assumption, common to all of those present, that there are rules requiring herdsmen to keep cattle away from crops and providing for compensation where damage is done in violation.

Something we take for granted in our own society is that different kinds of rule can be fairly readily distinguished. Rules of etiquette and good manners, ideal moral rules and rules of law are seen as occupying separate compartments, even if their reach may sometimes overlap. This kind of differentiation seems very rarely found in small-scale societies, and where indigenous distinctions are drawn their meanings should be studied very carefully before a classification based on our own system is imposed. Where detailed inventories of normative prescriptions are present, these are seldom classified in accordance with our own categories. This seems to be the case even in societies like the Tswana where vernacular words broadly corresponding to our 'law' are found.[4] The lack of a distinct

3. *Law without Precedent*, p. 320.
4. See p. 147 above.

category of legal rules does not imply that all rules have equal value and importance. In many societies some rules can be seen as carrying more weight in disputes than others; but even those most important rules are not 'especially organized for jural purposes' in quite the way that our legal rules are.[5] We should also remember that a distinction between the 'legal' and the 'political' forms a part of our own folk system in which their respective areas of operation are, at least on a superficial level, firmly marked out.

Where people do think and speak freely in normative terms, the clarity and detail vary greatly. In some societies norms tend to be vague and general, whereas in others they are precisely formulated and extend to considerable depth of detail. Terse comparisons capable of illustrating this point are hard to find, but useful examples are provided in the Ndendeuli, Arusha and Kgatla materials which we have already considered. Ndendeuli norms are rather general and imprecise, as we saw in that dispute over bridewealth and the duties of a son-in-law between Rajabu and Sedi.[6] While it is established that a Ndendeuli male who wishes to get married must present bride-wealth to his father-in-law, the amount that he must give, and even the nature of what he gives, remains uncertain. Over the years he may hand out sums of money and bolts of cloth; but these are also things which the good son-in-law would do for his wife's father even once he is married, so the dividing line between bridewealth payments and the duties owed by a son-in-law once the marriage is established is unclear. The Arusha bridewealth, on the other hand, ideally consists of a fixed number of cattle and smaller animals, every item of which is identified by its own name (e.g. *wakiteng* – an ox; *sotwa* – a female calf) and will be carefully 'ticked off' as it is presented.[7] At first sight it might seem that in this particular case the difference in clarity is related to the relative importance that these bridewealth payments hold in the two societies. (Certainly

5. Bohannan, *Justice and Judgment among the Tiv*, p. 58.
6. See p. 126 above.
7. Gulliver, *Social Control in an African Society*, p. 242.

more importance is attached to bridewealth among the Arusha.) However, this element of clarity runs right through the Arusha norms, whereas a corresponding lack of it is equally characteristic of the Ndendeuli. As well as being clear, Arusha norms vary in depth of detail, as we saw in Kadume's case: general rules like those prescribing harmony between agnates coexist with very detailed ones like those requiring that a man's field be inherited by his son. The Kgatla normative repertoire is even fuller and more readily expressed than that of the Arusha. They speak freely about approved rules of conduct, *mekgwa le melao ya Sekgatla*, and can provide instantly the appropriate rule to cover any factual situation. This repertoire they see as governing their everyday lives and providing guidelines in the case of dispute. As in the Arusha example, rules of different degrees of specificity coexist within the repertoire. These range from those of the greatest generality, which embody broad abstract principles upon which Kgatla society is based, to those specifying in tiny detail the kinds of redress that an individual may be entitled to in the event of some wrong being committed against him. An illustration may be taken from the rules relating to the devolution of property.[8] Here precise, substantive rules shade into prescriptions of a more general character, which in turn give way to precepts of a broad abstract kind. At the first of these levels are rules like those which require that the youngest son shall inherit the homestead of his mother; at an intermediate level are those like the one holding that instructions which a man gives as to the disposal of his property after he is dead must be obeyed (this principle is enshrined in the maxim *lentswe la moswi ga le tlolwe*: literally 'the voice of a dead man is not transgressed'); on the broadest level of generality are such rules as the one requiring that members of an agnatic group must live in peace with one another. Under these circumstances rules at different levels of specificity may be invoked so as to conflict with each other. For example, in a

8. Schapera, *A Handbook of Tswana Law and Custom*, pp. 230–38; Roberts and Comaroff, 'Chiefly Decision and the Devolution of Property in a Tswana Chiefdom', Cohen and Shack (eds.), *Politics in Leadership*.

dispute over a dwelling a youngest son seeking occupation might invoke the first, while the child of his father's brother might point to the third in justification of his own continued possession. In almost any such repertoire potentially conflicting rules may be discovered; a fact which has great importance for an understanding of how rules operate in the course of a dispute.

Finally, we shall notice in this context that apart from variations in clarity and depth of detail, rules may be *seen* to operate differently from one society to another. In the Kgatla case, for example, *mekgwa le melao ya Sekgatla* should be followed in everyday life, and where a dispute arises these rules provide the criteria whereby it is expected to be resolved; as the proverb quoted on page 147 indicates, even the chief is subject to these rules. Ideally, therefore, criteria such as political muscle are excluded when the outcome of a dispute has to be determined. The Arusha, on the other hand, have no less regard for their norms than the Kgatla. As Gulliver points out, it is these norms which give them their identity and make them different from the other peoples with whom they come into contact.[9] Yet they freely recognize that life does not work out strictly in accordance with rules, and that other criteria will also be important in governing the conduct of everyday affairs and in determining the outcome of a dispute. Furthermore, attitudes towards the breaking of rules in pursuit of individual interests can also be found to vary. In both Arusha and Kgatla society, norm-oriented conduct is always 'good' conduct. But this link is not universal, and some writers have gone so far as to contrast a 'norm-oriented' and a 'transactional' approach to life. Thus in one community conduct may be seen and tested on the basis of its correspondence to rules, while in others according to its utility in securing interests. As we saw in an earlier chapter, breaches of rules by 'big men' may attract approval; and it may even be by breaking rules that a man becomes 'big'.

These differences in the perception and use of normative

9. *Social Control in an African Society*, p. 241.

propositions in themselves suggest a variable relationship between rules and power, but it remains to be considered how far this relationship is linked to, and dependent upon, the form of governmental organization and modes of dispute settlement found in a given society. Here several writers have advanced some relatively simple principles which may be summarized as follows. Where centralized governments and adjudicatory processes of dispute settlement are found, rules are likely to be clear-cut and of crucial importance in decision-making, leaving little room for the operation of extra-normative criteria. On the other hand, in stateless societies where such settlement-directed talking as takes place is likely to be negotiatory, rules will be vague and of limited importance in reaching an outcome, leaving much greater play for pragmatic elements such as the physical, political and economic strength of the disputants.

As we saw in Chapter 9, it certainly seems to be the case that adjudicatory processes of settlement are largely confined to societies with some form of centralized organization. But how far can the remaining propositions be substantiated? Bohannan has argued that norms are likely to be ill-defined in stateless societies because in their case disputes tend to be settled by compromise which 'leads to very much less precise statements of norms as law than does the decision-based unicentric solution' associated with centralized systems.[10] At first sight this argument seems convincing, as in most centralized states rules *are* clear and detailed. The need for this to be so is plain, particularly in those cases where the state embraces a number of diverse ethnic groups. But one difficulty here is that there are acephalous societies in which rules are formulated with a precision similar to that found in centralized states. The Arusha, whose almost pedantically detailed rules about bridewealth we have already considered, provide an example of this. Further, any assumption that disputes are invariably resolved by compromise in acephalous societies and by decision in centralized states represents an over-simplification. As we have seen,

10. 'The Differing Realms of Law', *American Anthropologist*, Special Supplement, vol. 67, 33–42, p. 39.

processes of arbitration *are* sometimes found in stateless societies, and negotiatory processes are common at some levels in centralized states.

Gulliver advances much the same argument, but formulates it in a slightly different way when he suggests that[11] 'standards are both more vaguely defined and more flexible in areas of social life where negotiation procedures occur than in areas where adjudication is the mode'. Here again, the argument fits some of the data, particularly Gulliver's own Ndendeuli material, which he uses as his basis. It also avoids the second objection I raised to Bohannan's explanation. But like Bohannan's it cannot be reconciled with Gulliver's earlier description of Arusha dispute-settlement processes. Those findings might be consistent with a modified form of this hypothesis under which norms are postulated as vague in acephalous societies with relatively simple forms of organization like the Ndendeuli, rather more clear-cut in those with a complex organization like the Arusha, and most precise in the centralized state. However, even a formulation along those lines must run into difficulties when the detail and precision of normative prescriptions in Eskimo communities is remembered. Leaving that point aside, I would argue that an underlying problem with this kind of explanation is its assumption that rules *must* be vague when used in negotiatory processes if such processes are to be given the necessary flexibility to work. As we saw in connection with the Arusha material described in Chapter 7,[12] flexibility can be achieved otherwise than through vagueness of norm. The most precisely formulated rule may play a part in negotiatory processes provided it is understood, as it is in the Arusha case, that rules do not constitute the sole determinants of an outcome and that other criteria may play a part in the settlement process.

Whatever the conclusion on this part of the argument there remains the second limb, of greater importance for the present purposes, under which it is argued that rules are paramount

11. 'Case Studies of Law in Non-Western Societies', Nader (ed.), *Law in Culture and Society*, pp. 18–19.
12. See pp. 128–34 above.

under processes involving third-party decision, whereas under negotiatory processes disputes are resolved in accordance with the location of power between the two disputants. Again it is Gulliver who advances the argument in its bluntest form when he distinguishes between 'judicial' and 'political' means of resolving disputes: rule struggles and power struggles.[13] In scarcely less forthright terms Eckhoff characterizes the activities of judges as having to do with rules, and those of mediators as having to do with interests: 'The *judge* is distinguished from the mediator in that his activity is related to the level of norms rather than to the level of interests.'[14]

These arguments enjoy limited support to the extent that most accounts of adjudicatory processes lay greater emphasis on the part played by rules than is the case with descriptions of settlement by negotiation; but any terse opposition of rule and power, or rule and interest, must be misleading. Gulliver himself has now rejected the simple 'judicial'/'political' dichotomy which he earlier proposed: 'That is too simple as well as inaccurate. Even the idea of a continuum with pure judicial and pure political as polar opposites does not help. The political element is too pervasive for such treatment.'[15] At the same time, normative elements are seldom wholly excluded from negotiatory processes in the way Eckhoff's formulation suggests.

If we consider first those societies in which processes corresponding most closely to the judicial model may be found, and in which disputes are seen by the members as properly resolved in accordance with norms, there are several important ways in which political elements intrude. First, in many centralized states, those in power explicitly make rules and change them. A Kgatla chief is seen as having power to do this. Even if the rules are not 'made' by those in power they will be in a position to formulate and restate them. Secondly, in the Kgatla case, as

13. *Social Control in an African Society*, p. 297.
14. Eckhoff, 'The mediator, the judge and the administrator in conflict-resolution', Aubert (ed.), *Sociology of Law*, p. 175
15. 'Negotiations as a mode of dispute settlement: towards a general model', *Law and Society Review*, vol. 7, 667, 682.

elsewhere, those carrying out judicial functions at different levels in the society do so as representatives of the ruler. Although this feature is frequently contradicted or concealed in the ideology, Bohannan seems accurate when he defines a court as 'a body of men representative of the political power'.[16] Therefore, even if we see individual disputes as being resolved immaculately in accordance with norms, the political element is not removed, but merely raised to another level.

However, in practice political elements do also intrude to a greater or lesser degree in the resolution of individual disputes. One reason for this is that the repertoire of rules available in a given society never is, and hardly could be, an entirely consistent set. Rules can be adduced which conflict with each other, and those at different levels of generality can be juxtaposed in such a way that they appear contradictory. This is recognized even in a society like our own where 'legal rules' constitute a discrete sub-system. Elements of inconsistency and ambiguity must increase where 'legal rules' are not sharply distinguished from those of other normative orders. Further, in whatever detail rules are formulated they retain a 'general' character and have to be applied to the innumerable variations of actual human behaviour. Sometimes the 'fit' will be better than others, but in many cases in any system real doubt may be present as to whether a particular set of facts falls within a given rule. These characteristics of the rule-base enable disputants to 'fight' with rules in such a way that inherent inequalities are likely to affect the outcome of a dispute. The forceful and articulate man will be able to present his choice and formulation of the relevant rules more effectively than his reticent or inarticulate opponent. Where the presentation of disputes to the adjudicator is in the hands of specialists, the economic strength of the respective parties may similarly be reflected in the quality of the representation they are able to purchase. Such disparities can assume considerable importance, particularly when it is remembered that the umpire himself must fall back on criteria outside the system of rules in deciding the rule he must apply.

16. 'The Differing Realms of Law', *Law and Warfare*, p. 53.

Another opportunity for politics to enter the settlement process, even in a society with judicial institutions, is provided by the fact that resort to the solution provided by rule-based adjudication is never automatic. The range of possible responses to trouble is wide: the wrong may be allowed to pass unchallenged, or a remedy pursued through extra-judicial process on account of the publicity involved, the costs in time and material resources, or through the fear of further alienating a powerful adversary. All of these possibilities are open to exploitation by the actors and result in the intrusion of extra-normative criteria in the settlement process. For example, the poor man wronged by a wealthy neighbour may readily settle with him informally for much less than he might have gained in adjudication simply because his need is pressing and he is unable to sustain a lengthy dispute. Under such circumstances, the immediate offer of a couple of sheep may have to be accepted as a safer alternative to the several cows which might have been awarded later on. Here again, the inherent 'uncertainty' of any system of rule-based decision-making offers scope which the more powerful party may exploit.

Numerous other factors may be responsible for disparities being found between approved rules and observable human behaviour. Whatever the causes underlying this 'gap', its presence indicates an area of manoeuvre adjacent to the normative system within which interests may be pursued in accordance with criteria from outside the system. Individuals will inevitably differ markedly in the skill, energy and other resources through which this leeway can be exploited.

Despite the link which commentators have tended to make between centralized governmental organization and the authoritative operation of rules, there is no compelling reason why decision-making should be rule-based in a system where the ruler and his adjudicators have power to enforce their decisions. On the contrary, under these conditions the adjudicator is uniquely placed to reach any decisions he has to make on an arbitrary and *ad hoc* basis. Obviously over time such a practice might have implications for the adjudicator's legitimacy and survival; but the necessary link between third-party decision-making and rules, which Gulliver and Eckhoff seem to assume, is not established.

Thus it seems clear that there are ample opportunities for the exercise of power to intrude within systems where 'judicial' processes of decision-making operate. Nevertheless, these opportunities are certainly increased still further in processes of settlement by negotiation. Here, as we noted in Chapter 7, rules cannot even in theory *determine* outcome, for if they did the leeway essential in securing a compromise would be eliminated.

In the negotiatory processes we have already considered this political nature is further emphasized by the very way in which third parties intervene in them. We saw an example of this in the Arusha case where third parties align themselves in support groups behind the respective disputants. The need for such a partisan following is only there when non-normative criteria are seen to be applicable. The manner in which these support groups operate is plain from both the Ndendeuli and the Arusha cases which we have considered. The 'strength' of a disputant's position is determined in part from the size and quality of the support group he is able to convene. The man with a large group of prestigious, vociferous and articulate supporters begins with an inevitable advantage in the bargaining process. First, they promote his argument, speaking to it or chorusing their agreement with what they take to be its strong points; then, later, their support enables him to take a firm line in pursuing a favourable settlement. It is impossible to construe the support group's role as that of the neutral observer ensuring that approved norms are complied with in settlement. As Gulliver notes of the Arusha, they

are quite frank in admitting that support should, if necessary, be given to the extent of acting in what otherwise would be regarded as disapproved, unethical ways. As a conscious obligation, men may give false evidence or suppress pertinent but damaging evidence. It is an obligation not only to show up a fallacious argument or false evidence by the other disputant, but also deliberately to upset or confuse the other and his supporters by interruption, cross-questioning, twisting the argument, raising false issues or appealing to irrelevant emotion, precedence or other considerations.[17]

These Arusha processes are of an unambiguously political character, both in the sense that the strength of a man's following has crucial implications for the kind of settlement which he may achieve, and in the sense that without the support of his following the disputant has no chance of achieving a desired objective. It is also clear from Gulliver's descriptions that these groups, rather than the respective disputants, have ultimate control over the outcome which is eventually achieved. If there is a general consensus among all the supporters on both sides in favour of a particular solution, there is little that either disputant can do to fight against this. Where he attempts to do so he runs the risk that his supporters will simply melt away.

Gulliver's account also shows that, while the very structure of these processes results in the relative bargaining strength of the parties becoming an important determinant of the outcome, the Arusha themselves accept that other criteria than approved norms may be relevant in the attainment of a settlement, and that pragmatic arguments may be explicitly invoked.[18] They recognize that the simple need for peace and quiet against which the essential tasks of everyday life can go on may point towards a settlement quite different from that which might otherwise be demanded. Particularly where a disputant is faced with a stronger opponent whose continuing hostility may imperil his future interests, demands may be modified with a view to the maintenance of future cooperation; and the opponent himself will be fully alive to the tactical advantages he derives from such a situation and use his superior power to mould the outcome in his favour.

Despite these considerations we should not underestimate the part which rules play in processes of a mediatory or negotiatory character, and it certainly is not possible to accept without qualification Eckhoff's assertion that non-judicial processes are

17. *Social Control in an African Society*, p. 123.
18. ibid., pp. 241-2.

related to the 'level of interests'. In bilateral negotiation and in the course of mediation rules may be invoked and play an important part in shaping the outcome. In both of the disputes described in Chapter 7 (that between Rajabu and Sedi and that between Kadume and Soine) each side relied on and explicitly appealed to various norms in support of their respective arguments, and these norms influenced, without exclusively determining, the outcomes arrived at. In processes of this kind rules must be seen alongside pragmatic elements as counters in the bargaining process, and the relative 'normative strength' of each party may be of critical importance to the outcome. In both negotiatory and adjudicatory processes disputants may utilize rules in trying to make sure that their interests prevail in the contest. It is thus not a question of the presence or absence of rules in a particular kind of process but of the way in which rules are *used*. The ultimate difference between adjudicatory processes (where rules purport to be decisive) and negotiatory processes (where they cannot be) lies in the weight which may be attached in a dispute to this kind of weapon.

Finally we should also remember that even in those stateless societies where fighting, rather than some form of settlement-directed talking, constitutes a dominant mode of dispute settlement, the size and quality of the following which each disputant has managed to assemble may not be the sole determinant of the outcome. As we saw in the Maring and Minj-Wahgi examples referred to earlier, fighting may be highly formalized and subject to close normative regulation.[19]

When we consider the 'legal' and the 'political', and the relationship between rules and power, we must, therefore, start out from the position that all disputes are political in the sense that the disputants will be pursuing their respective interests in the face of inconsistent or competing claims. Beyond that, while any society must have some normative base, the extent to which norms are expressly articulated and compliance is emphasized in the value system will vary greatly. But a simple rule/power

19. See pp. 58 and 117–20 above.

dichotomy, which postulates societies in which order is maintained in accordance with a rigid application of rules and those where members conduct their affairs from first to last on a pragmatic basis, is no more than a caricature. Furthermore, while polarities of this kind have been quite widely invoked in attempts to identify the critical characteristics of different modes of dispute settlement, the route towards their understanding lies in comprehending the relationship of rules to power within a particular process, rather than characterizing it according to the purported presence or absence of one of these elements.

11

Main Themes and Interests in the Literature

At least since the publication in the mid-nineteenth century of Maine's famous work, *Ancient Law*, there has been wide interest in the 'law' of those societies which are smaller in scale and equipped with simpler governmental institutions and technology than our own. Nonetheless, while a large and scholarly literature has grown up, a reader fresh to the subject cannot help but notice how varied this work has been: for the most cursory survey reveals major differences of opinion about what should be studied, the methods to be followed in research, and the ways in which findings should be presented. This diversity is not surprising (much the same situation prevails in the areas of politics and religion); but it is hard for the newcomer to obtain a general picture of the subject within which individual works can be understood. This chapter is designed to provide such an overview by explaining the circumstances in which different kinds of work have been undertaken, indicating the way research method has developed and outlining some main theoretical concerns. It also provides an opportunity to draw together and place in context the interests we have been following so far.

As we saw in Chapter 2, there are two ways in which this subject has been viewed: as having to do with 'law'; or with broader issues of order in society. These perspectives are quite clearly reflected as diverging traditions in the literature; one formed of work which finds a theoretical base in western jurisprudence and another which disregards or even explicitly rejects this source. But beyond this major division, which has had implications both for the scope of an investigation and for the way in which the data were seen, the general objectives of research have varied widely. Perhaps a majority of studies have been conceived and carried out as contributions to scholarship, being designed to find out how continuity is maintained or disputes are settled in a given society, to relate these findings to reports from other societies and possibly to make some contribution to theory. Some studies, on the other hand, by both anthropologists and lawyers, have had the more mundane purpose of producing something of immediate practical use such as a handbook setting out the 'customary law' of a given tribe, for the use of officers responsible for its administration.

Similar variation is noticeable in the material upon which different studies have focused. Here three distinct orders of data have been taken by different scholars as the proper subject-matter of investigation: prescriptive rules; observable regularities in everyday human behaviour; and instances of dispute. A limited number of studies have conceded the importance of investigating each of these spheres concurrently if a properly rounded survey is to be made, but more often than not one dimension has been emphasized, and in some cases insufficient distinction has been drawn between data derived from these essentially different sources. Concurrent with such differences of focus have been variations in research strategy. Here the mode of collecting material has varied from the consultation of secondary sources (such as the writings of missionaries, explorers and administrators), through brief visits to the field in the course of which informants are questioned, to lengthy periods of participant-observation. The extent to which these variables may influence the ultimate product of research, irrespective of theoretical perspectives and the purpose for which the research is undertaken, can hardly be overemphasized.

Although problems of order in society have been of perennial interest to scholars, their explicit study in the context of small-scale societies began to develop only in the latter half of the nineteenth century. This was a time when efforts were being made to extend the application of evolutionary theory to fields outside biology, and a natural direction of these efforts lay in the social sciences, where one immediate concern was to chart the evolutionary steps through which the societies of contemporary Western Europe had passed. Because of obvious difficulties in tracing those early stages which were assumed to have been negotiated long ago, scholars turned for their material to those contemporary societies that seemed to represent these earlier stages in development. With the aid of such material, some scholars went so far as to postulate a single evolutionary scale along which all societies, from the most 'primitive' to the most 'advanced', could expect to pass. The growth of law and legal systems formed a very important part of these evolutionary schemes. This kind of theoretical perspective involved posing such questions as: 'Under what conditions, and at what stage in the evolutionary scale, does law emerge?' 'With what stages in human development are particular types of legal systems associated?' At this distance some of the answers to these questions, implicit in the various revolutionary schemes arrived at, may seem wrong and even absurd; but the questions were interesting ones, even if unhappily formulated and too readily linked with rigid evolutionary ideas. There were also considerable difficulties in answering such questions at that time. First, they were very large ones, and the knowledge then available about societies elsewhere in the world was much too thin to begin answering them. Secondly, the research strategies which had been developed at that time offered no means of obtaining such knowledge. Further, the questions were almost all formulated in an ethnocentric way which simply assumed that western legal categories offered an adequate analytical framework for understanding and organizing other peoples' concepts and institutions. As a single example, it was typically taken for granted that our categories of 'civil' and 'criminal' law were suitable for cross-cultural purposes.

The assumptions about social evolution that initially underlay questions relating to the circumstances under which 'law emerges' and to the different forms law may take under varied social conditions are well illustrated in the work of the English lawyer Sir Henry Maine. Maine's book *Ancient Law* appeared in 1861, and he is generally credited with having founded the area of study which has since become known as legal anthropology. Maine argued that human societies all passed through three basic stages of development. In the first of these stages, the largest grouping was made up of a few kinsmen, presided over by the senior male agnate. This man settled disputes and handed out punishments in the group but he did so on an *ad hoc* basis; no firm rules underpinned or connected the various decisions he took. At this stage law had yet to emerge. In the form of society which followed, numbers of these small groups of agnates became clustered together under chiefs, but the (sometimes fictional) assumption of shared kinship remained the basic organizing principle. Then came the territorial society, indicated by its identification with a particular tract of land. It was in the later part of the second stage and the early part of the third stage that 'law' began to develop, as the rulers started to pronounce the same judgements in similar situations, thus providing their decision-making with an underlying set of rules.

A normative basis for decision-making was the key attribute of law for Maine. Later in the development of territorial societies, the handling of disputes fell into the hands of a specialized élite, who alone had access to the principles to be followed in their resolution. As Maine wrote: 'What the juristical oligarchy now claims is to monopolize the *knowledge* of the laws, to have the exclusive possession of the principles by which quarrels are decided'.[1] Later still, to ensure accurate knowledge of the rules, and to avoid the distrust resulting from them being the exclusive property of legal specialists, they were written down into codes. During this 'era of codes' a final development began. As societies changed, the demand came that the laws should change with them. Some societies developed devices for altering the rigid codes as this became necessary; others failed to do so. Thus, the territorial society

1. *Ancient Law*. The quotation is from the Everyman's Library Edition (1917), p. 7.

could take on alternative forms, the 'stationary' or the 'progressive'. Within and alongside this overall evolutionary framework for the legal system, Maine also postulated evolutionary sequences through which different areas of the substantive law, such as contract and the criminal law, would develop.

Although Maine later denied that he had ever contemplated a single path of development, through successive stages of which each society had to pass, *Ancient Law* gives a very strong impression of having been written on the assumption of a unilineal developmental course (at least until the parting of the ways between progressive and stationary societies). But this evolutionary cast does not detract from the importance of the questions he was asking as to the origins of 'law' and the relationship between different forms of law and social organization. Further, the answers he provided were of striking interest considering that he had little data before him apart from that to be drawn from Greece, Rome and some Indian civilizations.

Maine was not alone in pursuing these large questions about the growth of law and legal systems in an evolutionary context. In America, Morgan produced a vastly elaborate scheme at about the same time[2] and similar work was undertaken by German legal ethnologists. Maine was followed in England by others who produced far more detailed and complex evolutionary schemes of social growth on to which were grafted corresponding frameworks of legal development.[3] Émile Durkheim also associated successive forms of social organization with different types of legal system. Indeed, it was through legal forms that he purported to test his famous hypothesis concerning the relationship of 'mechanical' and 'organic' solidarity. Societies in which mechanical solidarity prevailed basically exhibited 'repressive' sanctions, while those in which organic solidarity had developed were characterized by 'restitutive' sanctions. By establishing what type of law predominated in a given society, Durkheim argued, you could therefore ascertain that society's basic nature.[4]

2. *Ancient Society.*
3. For instance Hobhouse, *Morals in Evolution.*
4. *The Division of Labour in Society.*

Most of these earliest speculations were carried out from a position of almost complete ignorance as to the actual organization of the simpler societies then existing in Africa, Asia and the Pacific; information about them was simply not available. By the end of the nineteenth century, with increasing missionary activity and the process of colonial expansion, more was becoming known. But research methods remained of a very restricted kind. Most scholars relied for their material on 'primitive law' upon the accounts of travellers, missionaries and colonial administrators whose works were seldom written directly with a view to answering the questions in which the scholars were interested. It was still quite rare for ethnographers to go into the field themselves. The story has often been told of Sir James Frazer, who, when once asked whether he had ever met any of the people he wrote about, replied, 'God forbid!' Nevertheless, by the end of the nineteenth century it was becoming recognized that there was no satisfactory alternative to the scholar going himself into the field and collecting his information directly. But this still did not entail sustained observation of the processes of everyday life; instead it depended upon obtaining a reliable paid informant, preferably of the tribe concerned, who would then be subjected to severe cross-examination as to what the members of his tribe did and believed. The early motion pictures of Dr Carl Gustave Jung examining (and paying) informants while seated under a cork helmet at a picnic table convey very well the essence of these occasions. They were typically conducted through an interpreter, and the preconceptions and enthusiasms of the scholar, combined with the fears and desire to please of the informant, made the reliability of information collected by these methods very doubtful.

Notwithstanding the limitations of research method, two important features of these societies were already clear by the early years of this century. One of these was that, even in the very simplest groups that had been discovered, there were socially accepted rules which people generally followed in everyday life. There was not, as had sometimes been postulated, a state of brutal anarchy, with 'every one against every one'.

The other was that in most of these societies there was no-one in a position to enforce the rules; often no chiefs, let alone courts and police apparatus. This presence of order but absence of enforcement agencies led people to ask such questions as: 'How is order maintained in such societies?' 'Why are the rules obeyed if there is no-one to enforce them?' Initial answers suggested that the rules were followed 'automatically', as a matter of course; that 'the savage ... is bound in the chains of immemorial tradition'.[5] Rivers, in his book *Social Organisation*, suggested: 'Among such a people as the Melanesians there is a group sentiment which makes unnecessary any definite social machinery for the exertion of authority ...'[6] From being primitive anarchists who freely indulged their slightest impulses, members of these societies came to be seen as automata.

Malinowski's work, published following extensive fieldwork in the Trobriand Islands, can now be seen as a turning point in the study of 'primitive law'. He started out asking the same questions as scholars like Rivers and Hartland, in that he was interested in the way in which acephalous societies managed to hold together – without 'courts and constables', as he put it. But both in the way he went about finding the answers, and in the conclusions he came up with, his approach was startlingly different.

In order to conduct his research he pitched his tent in the middle of a village of Trobriand fishermen and started to observe what was going on around him. While this procedure now seems to us preferable to cross-examining a few carefully chosen informants at a safe distance, it then represented a revolutionary strategy. It also opened up new possibilities in terms of the results achieved. For instead of being limited to idealized statements of rules, and second-hand reports of what people did and said, the researcher could obtain a direct view of regularities in everyday behaviour and of what actually happened when a quarrel broke out.

5. Hartland, *Primitive Law*, p. 138.
6. p. 169.

As a result of his research in the Trobriands, Malinowski offered a very different explanation of how such societies held together from the one provided by scholars like Rivers. On the basis of his observations he suggested that order in these societies was *not* something automatically present, but that it was secured by a range of ever-present checks upon human conduct. We have already considered what he took these mechanisms to be in the Trobriand case. Here it is important to note simply that in offering a different interpretation of order in these societies to those which were currently fashionable he insisted on the need to get away from a preoccupation with western institutional forms. We have already quoted him as saying: 'law ought to be defined by function and not by form, that is, we ought to see what are the arrangements, the sociological realities, the cultural mechanisms which act for the enforcement of law' (see p. 28 above). This message is a simple one but it is of great importance: we should look for the means whereby order and continuity are maintained, and in doing so should not necessarily hope to find these in the context of familiar institutional forms.

Both Malinowski's research strategy, and the novel perspective on questions of order which he advocated, proved immensely influential with other scholars. It would not be an exaggeration to say that his work represented a watershed in the study of social control in small-scale societies. Following his work an entirely new line of research developed under which problems of order and conflict were considered in a way which escaped the constricting framework of western jurisprudence. The old law-centred studies were not discontinued, in fact they flourished for reasons which will be considered below; but after Malinowski they were accompanied by a parallel stream of great vigour which derived little of its impetus from legal theory. The subsequent growth of these respective traditions will be considered separately here.

LAW-CENTRED STUDIES

Despite the wide interest which *Crime and Custom in Savage Society* provoked, legal theory continued to provide the framework within which some studies of order and dispute in small-scale societies were undertaken. This jurisprudential influence can be seen in definitions of law formulated for cross-cultural purposes which still emphasized familiar hallmarks of our own system – rules, courts and organized force. For example, in his now classical discussion of 'primitive law' Radcliffe-Brown explicitly adopted the lawyer Roscoe Pound's formulation of law as 'social control through the systematic application of the force of politically organized society'.[7] Similarly, Evans-Pritchard identified law with a situation where there is some 'authority with power to adjudicate' and to 'enforce a verdict'.[8]

These formulations were reflected in numerous field studies produced during the 1930s and 40s which presented the 'law' of small-scale societies as an affair of rules, courts and enforcement agencies, the whole operating very much in the manner of our own legal system. Such studies almost invariably consisted of inventories of recorded rules organized and presented in categories corresponding closely to those of common law and civil law systems. The assumption seems to be made in the majority that this normative material bears the characteristics of legal rules, and that individual norms are effective to determine the outcome of disputes in which they are invoked.

The main stimulus towards the survival of studies of this kind can be found in the task of administering a colonial empire. Although the system of Indirect Rule, under which the indigenous population of a colonized territory was largely governed through 'native' intermediaries, had been officially established throughout the British African possessions and dependencies by the early 1930s, the activities of these intermediaries still had to be supervised by expatriate administrative

7. 'Primitive Law', *Encyclopaedia of the Social Sciences*, vol. 9, 202–6, p. 202.

8. *The Nuer*, p. 162.

officers. In the context of the law-enforcement side of government, such supervision involved the officers both in hearing appeals from the decisions of 'native courts' and undertaking periodic reviews of the business which these dispute-settlement agencies dealt with. These functions necessitated some knowledge of the 'native law and custom' concerned. In many cases this had to be acquired by experience, but in a number of territories manuals were published which purported to provide an account of the 'laws and customs' concerned, either in narrative form or in some rule-by-rule format. The best of these was Schapera's now classic work, *A Handbook of Tswana Law and Custom*; but on the whole they were of varied quality and many were not prepared by professional anthropologists.

It does not necessarily follow from the fact that a scholar has formulated an ethnocentric definition of law that he allows this to colour his understanding of the concepts, institutions and processes of the society he is observing. This point is neatly illustrated by Evans-Pritchard's work among the Nuer, which we considered in an earlier chapter.[9] Having formulated his definition he at once conceded that 'In a strict sense Nuer have no law',[10] stopped worrying about this, and went on to describe very successfully how these people nonetheless managed to live a relatively ordered social life and handle instances of conflict when these arose. All too frequently, however, the ill-effects of a grounding in western legal theory do become apparent in empirical studies. The precise manner in which jural influences obtrude varies but two obvious pitfalls may be identified.

The first of these is inherent in the effort to isolate 'legal' data for separate examination which is characteristic of law-centred studies. Given the nature of social control institutions in small-scale societies such works must necessary involve ultimately unsatisfactory efforts to extract differentiated legal material from an undifferentiated mass of data found in the society concerned. Apart from the fact that the material chosen for extraction must suffer in the process of being cast in a differen-

9. See pp. 120–21 above.
10. *The Nuer*, p. 162.

tiated form, the overall value of the study is almost inevitably diminished through one type of control institution being investigated in isolation from others of potentially equal importance to which its operations are intimately related. The method involves inclusion and exclusion on a basis which is not necessarily meaningful in the society concerned. There is then often the temptation to label the material excluded as pre-legal, thus implying some quite unproven evolutionary process towards 'law'.

The second difficulty relates to the distortion which takes place when the material chosen for exposition is compressed into a 'legal' mould. Here the risk of distortion arises when undifferentiated normative data are invested with attributes of legal rules and a firmly judicial character is impressed upon all forms of third-party intervention. All rules are treated as legal rules, and all peace-makers are identified as 'judges'.

In Africa a new impetus was given to such studies during the pre-independence period following the Second World War. At this time, throughout the existing British African territories there was a movement towards 'integrating' the traditional 'courts' (which had survived under the system of Indirect Rule) more closely with those of the national legal system.[11] This move was seen to require the clarification and, in the view of some, the unification of the different systems of rules which these agencies were applying in the dispute-settlement process. One programme established in response to this demand was the Restatement of African Law Project of the School of Oriental and African Studies, University of London. This Project, which was initiated in 1959 and drew a significant number of lawyers into this area of study for the first time, aimed to 'record the customary law' of those traditional African societies which survived within modern national boundaries and to prepare 'restatements' of this material suitable for use in the newly

11. Two useful general sources on this development are: Allott (ed.), *The Future of Law in Africa*; Twining, *The Place of Customary Law in the National Legal Systems of East Africa*.

integrated courts.[12] The reports of the Project consist largely of inventories of rules purporting to constitute the 'customary law' of each society investigated. But the process whereby these rules, extracted from undifferentiated normative data, were selected for inclusion is not explicit. Nor is much explanation offered of how they actually work in the society concerned. The reader is left with the impression, presumably shared by those who prepared the restatements, that they operate in the same way as rules of English law are conventionally seen to operate: as determining the outcome of disputes arising within the area of behaviour to which they apply. Further, the categories within which these rules are organized are those of English law. Although the authors of the Project note the need to develop 'suitable categories of analysis and description' there is no indication in the published reports that this vital step was undertaken.

The work of the Restatement Project may be an extreme example in the sense that efforts were made to organize normative material in a rigid rule-by-rule format. But it is entirely representative in that it exhibits openly the assumption underlying a whole tradition of scholarship by lawyers: that material found in these societies is susceptible to the forms of analysis employed by lawyers within their own system. Many works have appeared in the last two decades, particularly in Africa, which assume that 'customary law' can be treated in this way. Such works continue to be published and in terms of legal scholarship some are of very high quality, but they are all flawed by an underlying assumption that the material they are dealing with can safely be submitted to those forms of analysis which lawyers use upon English law. This assumption, as we saw in Chapter 2, can seldom be made.

Some anthropologists also remained strongly influenced by western jurisprudence during the post-war period. This influence can be found both in their continuing determination to define 'law' for cross-cultural purposes, and in the substance of the

12. Allott, Introduction to Cotran, *Kenya I: The Law of Marriage and Divorce*, vol. 1 in the Restatement of African Law Series.

definition which they eventually arrived at. Hoebel, for example, committed himself to the view that 'for working purposes law may be defined in these terms: *A social norm is legal if its neglect or infraction is regularly met, in threat or in fact, by the application of physical force by an individual or group possessing the socially recognized privilege of so acting.*'[13] With even closer fidelity to western legal theory of a positivist kind, Pospisil sees law as 'principles abstracted from legal decisions', and insists that a decision must have four essential 'attributes' if it is to be considered legal: authority, intention of universal application, *obligatio*, and sanction.[14] A recent definition by Bohannan portrays law as consisting of rules which have become institutionalized through their presence in social forms, and then 're-institutionalized' through their enforcement by legal institutions. 'Legal institutions' are those agencies which settle disputes and deal with serious abuses of rule.[15] He thus implies the presence of a specialized subsystem of the kind which is present in our own society. In this formulation he seems very close to that of Hart which we have already considered;[16] it similarly presents considerable difficulties of application in many of the societies we are concerned with.

These theoretical perspectives are inevitably reflected in some of the empirical studies which appeared in the 1950s and 60s. A good example is provided by Pospisil's own field study, *Kapauku Papuans and Their Law*, a telling result of the theories just outlined. Although Pospisil is careful to outline the social context in which 'Kapauku law' operates, it is nonetheless presented as a catalogue of rules possessing a strongly 'legal' character. This is inevitably so as he defines law as 'principles extracted from legal decisions' and insists that these rules operate in a manner corresponding closely to that contemplated

13. *The Law of Primitive Man*, p. 28 (italics in original).

14. *Anthropology of Law*, pp. 39–96.

15. 'The Differing Realms of Law', *American Anthropologist*, Special Supplement, vol. 67, 33–42.

16. See p. 24 above.

in the more formalistic accounts of the English judicial system. To sustain this argument he is obliged to force the Kapauku 'big man' into a rigid judicial mould. However, judging by Pospisil's own case data and from accounts of similar Papuan communities, it is hard to avoid the conclusion that his presentation of the 'big men' in a judicial role owes more to Pospisil's preconceived ideas about the nature of law than to the realities of the Kapauku dispute-settlement process. It is fair to say that work by anthropologists in this tradition is becoming rare, but it does continue to appear.

Although as we have seen, there are great difficulties in the way of presenting 'law' in these societies as an affair of rules and courts, it would be quite wrong to adopt a dismissive attitude towards all the research which has adhered to the legal tradition. Two works, particularly, while themselves remaining within a law-centred frame, have had an immensely important influence upon broader studies of social control. These are *The Cheyenne Way*, by Llewellyn and Hoebel, and *The Judicial Process among the Barotse of Northern Rhodesia*, by Gluckman. Both have a distinctly 'legal' flavour in that they are concerned with how legal rules are formulated and changed and with how disputes are 'judged'; but both in their different ways pushed the subject forward in important directions. *The Cheyenne Way* represented a complete break with earlier studies in that Llewellyn and Hoebel directed their attention towards the intensive study of disputes. While Malinowski had been interested in quarrels and how they were resolved, most of his material related to regularities observable in everyday life and to the mechanisms securing the order which this regularity represented. Llewellyn and Hoebel filled this gap by insisting on the importance of examining instances of dispute and showing what could be wrung out of them through skilful analysis. Gluckman was also concerned with disputes, the importance of his work lying in his exploration of the character of rules and the manner in which these might be used in decision-making.

STUDIES OF ORDER AND DISPUTE

Following Malinowski there also appeared a range of studies concerned with problems of order and conflict, rather than that segment of the subject which could be identified with the 'legal' (significantly, the word 'law' is rarely used in many of these works). The precise scope and focus of these studies has been extremely varied, beyond the shared escape from the constraints of legal scholarship. One early work was Evans-Pritchard's *Witchcraft, Oracles and Magic among the Azande*, a central concern of which was with the control implications of witchcraft and sorcery practices. Others have ranged over such diverse matters as: processes of socialization;[17] the handling of dispute through armed combat;[18] the control implications of various ritual procedures, including competitive exchanges of food;[19] and the management of quarrels generated in the course of struggles for political leadership.[20] Alongside these have been studies which have concentrated upon processes of settlement-directed discussion, some of a relatively 'court-like' nature.[21]

Despite these differences, the works we are now considering shared several distinctive features. First, and inevitably given the rejection of a legal mould, was the common concern with finding a suitable framework for comprehending and describing alien institutions of social control. While a clear recognition of the dangers inherent in fitting the features of the society under observation, consciously or unconsciously, into a conceptual and institutional framework derived from one to which the observer belongs is implicit in his writing, Malinowski does not state this expressly. It was left to Bohannan to discuss these problems explicitly, in the context of the study of social control, in his book *Justice and Judgment among the Tiv*. There he

17. Berndt, *Excess and Restraint*.
18. Koch, *War and Peace in Jalemo*.
19. Young, *Fighting with Food*.
20. Turner, *Schism and Continuity in an African Society*.
21. See, for instance, Gulliver's works: *Social Control in an African Society; Neighbours and Networks*.

warned against the anthropologist allowing preconceptions about law in his own society to colour his description of what he saw in the society under investigation, and also stressed the need for this description to contain an account of the way in which the members of that society themselves understood and explained what they said and did ('the folk system'). Any analytical frame subsequently constructed for the purpose of comparison ('the analytical system') should, as far as possible, constitute a neutral model, not derived directly from any one society. In this way, the anthropologist could guard against the danger 'that he will change one of the folk systems of his own society into an analytical system and give it wider application than its merit and usefulness allow'.[22] Although on the face of it the points which Bohannan is making might seem simple and uncontroversial, extensive argument followed on his attempts to elaborate these ideas.[23] Indeed, the fiercest debates conducted in this area of study during the 1960s concerned problems of how far, and in what way, ethnocentric bias could be avoided and of the use best made of 'native' concepts and categories.

Another distinguishing characteristic of these studies was their primary concern with *processes* rather than with the analysis of institutions or the formulation of rules. In part this change of perspective flowed naturally from the adoption of participant-observation as the principal research method. But it must also be seen in the context of that broad movement in the social sciences associated with such labels as game theory and transactional analysis (a development that was itself anticipated by Malinowski in his preoccupation with the way in which Trobrianders exploited their relationships of reciprocal obligation). This shift showed itself in a growing interest in what individuals did and in how actors themselves understood and explained their behaviour. Rules and institutional forms remained of interest, but only in so far as they illuminated observed regularities or instances of dispute.

22. p. 5.
23. See p. 17 and the accompanying footnote.

Most of these studies also revealed an entirely different view of conflict to the one which characterized law-centred works. In them disputes were seen as a normal and inevitable part of social life; as channels through which existing social forms might be reproduced and through which change could be negotiated. Because the dispute ceased to be seen as a pathological event, it was no longer regarded as capable of being neatly excised from the rest of life for individual scrutiny, but had to be treated as an integral part of the life of the community in which it took place. It followed from such a perspective that where a dispute was investigated, the inquiry was not limited to the narrow 'slice' represented by proceedings before court-like agencies, but widened to embrace consideration of the whole ambit of conflict, including the genesis of the trouble, successive attempts to resolve it (whatever their nature) and the subsequent history of relations between the parties involved. Related to this was a movement away from treating a single dispute as the basic unit of investigation. Scholars like Turner and Gulliver stressed the need to comprehend a whole sequence of quarrels taking place in a given community over time if individual elements in the picture were to be properly understood. They showed that in small face-to-face communities one dispute was intimately related to those which came before it, and itself determined important features of any which followed. Patterns of alliance altered over successive instances of conflict and the strategies and outcome observed in a given case had meaning only in the light of what had gone before.

These important changes in direction brought with them a view of rules and dispute settlement quite different to that adopted in law-centred studies. Rules were no longer seen as crisply determining outcomes, and in so far as they were seen as important at all they were treated as a resource which disputants and third parties might draw upon in pursuing a quarrel. At the same time, the rigid judicial model of third-party intervention was abandoned, and the role of such figures as go-betweens and mediators in the settlement process began to be considered. Even in societies exhibiting relatively court-like processes of settlement, the new studies concentrated on exploring the role which intervening third parties *actually performed* in settlement, whether as partisan, mediator, umpire or otherwise. Such studies paved the way for the development of typologies of different modes of intervention, and the formation of hypotheses as to the circumstances under which such different modes would be encountered.

So far as the disputant himself was concerned, attention now began to be given to the way he behaved in the course of a quarrel: what his objectives were in pursuing it; the ways in which he recruited support; the manner in which he chose the agency before which he brought the dispute for settlement; and the tactics he adopted before that agency. One feature which was stressed again and again was the strong element of compromise which tended to be present in any given outcome and which gave the dispute-settlement process a 'bargaining' flavour markedly different from the 'zero-sum game' of win-or-lose adjudication under the common law model. Overall, this new emphasis on the bargaining, transactional side of life provided a valuable complement to the view which sees order in terms of application of rules and obedience to them.

No less important were those contemporary studies, predominantly dealing with Melanesian societies, which turned away from settlement-directed talk altogether and concerned themselves with other modes of handling conflict, notably fighting and sorcery.[24] Something which emerged from these studies was that trouble seemed to lead to violent self-help much more easily in some kinds of acephalous society than in others. This finding set in train speculation as to why some modes of settlement were dominant in one society and not in another; or put in a more loaded way, why was talking as a mode of settlement 'better established' in some societies than in others?

24. See, for instance, Koch, *War and Peace in Jalemo*; Young, *Fighting with Food*; Rappaport, *Pigs for the Ancestors: Ritual in the Ecology of a New Guinea People*.

Through those studies which dwelt on fighting rather than talking a legal distinction of long standing between questions of the internal regulation of a society, and of the handling of its external relations, was thrown over. For, again particularly in Melanesian societies, research showed that even within a homogeneous ethnic group discrete communities might be found which behaved towards each other very much as two nation states might behave, enjoying successive periods of peace and war. So the old 'law/war' dichotomy which had previously marked out mutually exclusive areas of interest becomes of doubtful value.

It is also of interest that the theoretical concerns pursued in these contemporary studies come very close to those of the nineteenth-century scholars referred to at the beginning of this chapter. Armed with much fuller and more accurate data anthropologists are now turning back to the large and important questions which were then boldly asked but have remained since without wholly satisfying answers. It is now possible to reconsider such general questions as: 'How is order maintained in stateless societies?' 'What kind of control mechanisms should we expect to be associated with different forms of social organization?' 'Are there observable patterns underlying the way in which control mechanisms change in a society over time?' Thus, some old problems are being considered afresh, with fuller material and stripped of the constraints imposed by any rigid evolutionary frame.

At this point it is necessary to consider how rigid is the divide between these apparently disparate traditions in the literature and whether there can be any future meeting point between them. Experience does not provide the basis for much optimism, as past debate across this boundary has generated some of the most wasteful and debilitating quarrels within the discipline.

At some levels the divergence is irreducible. Proponents of law-centred studies confine their attention to one particular mode of social action which they see as manifesting itself in recognizable, if slightly varying, forms across a range of societies. In doing so they necessarily restrict the area of investigation to the nature and operation of a special category of rules and decision-making processes. As we have seen, the interests of the rival tradition vary widely beyond a shared concern with questions of order and dispute; but they have in common the view that it is not feasible or desirable to isolate the 'legal' as a generic field of study.

Unfortunately much of the debate across the line has involved questioning the legitimacy and value of the respective traditions of study rather than a search for common ground. A principal criticism levelled by the supporters of law-centred studies is that the others cast the net too wide, causing the rigour of the study to be lost.[25] One wrote recently of the 'desert of social control', implying that the area was arid as well as easy to get lost in.[26] Another much more specific criticism is that a concern with behaviour, particularly with the way in which people pursue 'interests', leads the essential normative character of control mechanisms to be overlooked.[27] In the other direction a major objection to the law-centred studies has been that mechanisms of control, however specialized, do not operate in isolation, and that to segregate them for the purposes of study can only lead to distortion. As we saw in Chapter 2, some people have also been worried that a concern with the 'legal' can too easily lead to damaging attempts to fit indigenous data into alien categories.

The weight to be attached to any one of these arguments must depend upon the exact context in which it is made and upon the particular work against which it is directed. Nonetheless, two points may be made concerning law-centred studies in general. First, all those scholars who insist that we should treat law as a 'specific mode of social action' make assumptions about the nature of the 'legal' which have their

25. See, for instance, Redfield, 'Primitive Law', Bohannan (ed.), *Law and Warfare*.

26. Hamnett, *Chieftainship and Legitimacy*, p. 103.

27. ibid.

origins in our own folk categories. Secondly, in none of their work is a fundamental question answered: What do we gain by insisting that particular arrangements should be characterized as 'legal', whereas others should not? It remains unclear how the use of this label can help us in the essential task of understanding what particular institutions look like, how particular processes work, and the ways in which these are to be distinguished analytically from those found in other contexts.

Whatever side we may take in this controversy, one very striking fact about it is worth mentioning. This concerns the kinds of societies which the protagonists on either side have studied. The most casual examination of the literature confirms that, apart from Pospisil, those writers who advocate a law-centred approach have done their research in societies with some form of centralized political organization and dispute-settlement agencies in which clear adjudicatory processes are observable: here the work of scholars like Gluckman and Fallers provides obvious examples. Whereas those in opposition have all worked in acephalous societies, a number of them in groups where settlement-directed talking seems scarcely followed, and none in groups where adjudicatory procedures are established. Here scholars like Berndt, Bohannan, Gulliver, Koch, Turner and Young come to mind. The fact that the kind of material which a particular writer had to work with has so extensively intruded on the discussion lends an air of unreality to the debates and suggests that a lot of the argument was never really joined.

If we are to look for some common ground this must lie at those points where the interest in rules and institutions exhibited in law-centred studies can complement the concern with processes and with what individuals are actually doing, shown in broader studies of order. As became clear in earlier chapters, one such point may be found in the further study of settlement procedures. We still know very little about the different forms which settlement-directed talking may take, and the conditions under which these forms are likely to be encountered. Here progress may only be made through interest in process and institutional form coinciding.

Another area in which the two approaches could be valuably combined concerns the understanding of how rules operate, and their relationship to the pursuit of interests and the exercise of power. Hitherto rules and power have too often been considered apart. Law-centred studies have focused upon the ways in which rules delimit the shape of institutions, prescribe courses of conduct and determine outcomes; or, following Durkheim, reflect particular social forms. On the other hand, other studies have tended to neglect rules in considering the way people order their affairs and try to secure their interests. We can learn much more about how rules work and how power is exercised if a centre of attention becomes the way in which actors see rules and use them in protecting their interests and pursuing disputes. In this context there is a strong argument for looking much more closely than has generally been the case at what people say and how they say it in the conduct of disputes. Talking, as Bloch has recently reminded us,[28] provides one of the most important vehicles through which people try to exercise control over each other. It is also on occasions of dispute that important rules are most likely to be articulated and re-formulated.

The manner in which rules are perceived and manipulated also remains an essential area of investigation if we are to address crucial questions touching the relationship between rules and human behaviour: 'Why do people obey rules?' 'Under what circumstances do rules acquire, retain or lose social acceptance?' These questions are of theoretical interest to anthropologists whether they are working upon the control institutions of an acephalous society or on those of a centralized state with a differentiated legal system. They are also of concern to lawyers whether working in a developing country or an industrialized nation. In any society statutory innovation and creative judicial activity must remain uncertain exercises until we know more about the answers to them. The difficul-

28. *Political Language and Oratory in Traditional Society.*

ties are particularly acute in a plural society where the national legal system has been superimposed on the normative systems of several diverse ethnic groups. And here we may conclude by remembering that the societies we have been considering in this book are now to be found – those of them that survive in an identifiable form – within the context of some larger nation-state and subject to its legal system.

Bibliography

ABEL, R. L. 'The Comparative Study of Dispute Institutions in Society', *Law and Society Review*, vol. 8 (1973), 217–347.

ALLOTT, A. N. (ed.) *The Future of Law in Africa* (London, 1959).

AUBERT, V. (ed.) *Sociology of Law* (London, 1969).

AUSTIN, J. *The Province of Jurisprudence Determined* (London, 1832).

BARTH, F. *Political Leadership among the Swat Pathans* (London, 1959).

BERNDT, R. M. *Excess and Restraint* (Chicago, 1962).

BLACK-MICHAUD, J. *Cohesive Force: Feud in the Mediterranean and the Middle East* (London, 1975).

BLOCH, M. (ed.) *Political Language and Oratory in Traditional Society* (London, 1975).

BOHANNAN, P. J. *Justice and Judgment among the Tiv* (London, 1957).

BOHANNAN, P. J. (ed.) *Law and Warfare* (New York, 1967).

BOHANNAN, P. J. 'The Differing Realms of Law', *American Anthropologist*, Special Supplement, vol. 67 (1965), 33–42; also in *Law and Warfare*.

BURRIDGE, K. 'Disputing in Tangu', *American Anthropologist*, vol. 59, no. 5 (1957), 763–80.

CODÈRE, H. *Fighting with Property* (New York, 1950).

COLSON, E. 'Social Control and Vengeance in Plateau Tonga Society', *Africa*, vol. 23 (1953), 199–212.

COLSON, E. *The Plateau Tonga of Northern Rhodesia: Social and Religious Studies* (Manchester, 1962).

COMAROFF, J. L. 'Rules and Rulers: Political Processes in a Tswana Chiefdom', *Man* (N.S.), vol. 13 (1978), pp. 1–20.

COMAROFF, J. L. with ROBERTS, S. 'The Invocation of Norms in Dispute Settlement: The Tswana Case', HAMNETT (ed.), *Social Anthropology and Law*, London, 1977).

CORY, H. *Sukuma Law and Custom* (London, 1953).

COTRAN, E. *Kenya I: The Law of Marriage and Divorce*, vol. 1 in the Restatement of African Law Series (London, 1968).

DEMERATH, N. J. (ed.) with PETERSON, R. A. *System, Change and Conflict: A Reader in Sociological Theory and the Debate about Functionalism* (Glencoe, 1968).

DIVALE, W. T. with CHAMBERIS, F. and GANGLOFF, D. 'War, Peace, and Marital Residence in Pre-Industrial Societies', *Journal of Conflict Resolution*, vol. 20 (1976), 57–78.

DURKHEIM, É. *The Division of Labour in Society* (New York, 1947); published in French 1893.

ECKHOFF, T. 'The mediator, the judge and the administrator in conflict-resolution', *Acta Sociologica*, vol. 10 (1966), 148–72.

EPSTEIN, A. L. (ed.) *Contention and Dispute* (Canberra, 1974).

EVANS-PRITCHARD, E. *The Nuer* (Oxford, 1940).

EVANS-PRITCHARD, E. *Witchcraft, Oracles and Magic among the Azande.* (Oxford, 1937).

FALLERS, L. Law without Precedent (Chicago, 1969).

FRANK, J. *Law and the Modern Mind* (New York, 1930).

FREUCHEN, P. *Arctic Adventure* (New York, 1935).

GELLNER, E. *Saints of the Atlas* (London, 1969).

GIBBS, J. L. 'The Kpelle Moot: A Therapeutic Model for the Informal Settlement of Disputes', *Africa*, vol. 33 (1963), 1–11.

GLUCKMAN, M. 'Gossip and Scandal', *Current Anthropology*, vol. 4 (1963), 307–16.

GLUCKMAN, M. *Politics, Law and Ritual in Tribal Society* (London, 1965).

GLUCKMAN, M. *The Judicial Process among the Barotse of Northern Rhodesia* (Manchester, 1955).

GRINNELL, G. B. *The Cheyenne Indians* (New Haven, 1923).

GULLIVER, P. H. 'Case Studies of Law in Non-Western Societies', NADER (ed.), *Law in Culture and Society*.

GULLIVER, P. H. 'Negotiations as a mode of dispute settlement: towards a general model', *Law and Society Review*, vol. 7 (1973), 682.

GULLIVER, P. H. *Neighbours and Networks* (Berkeley, 1971).

GULLIVER, P. H. *Social Control in an African Society* (London, 1963).

HAMNETT, I. *Chieftainship and Legitimacy* (London, 1975).

HART, H. L. A. *The Concept of Law* (Oxford, 1961).

HARTLAND, S. *Primitive Law* (London, 1924)

HIATT, L. R. *Kinship and Conflict: A Study of an Aboriginal Com-*

munity in Northern Arnhem Land (Canberra, 1965).

HOBBES, T. *Leviathan* (London, 1651).

HOBHOUSE, L. T. *Morals in Evolution* (London, 1906).

HOEBEL, E. A. *The Law of Primitive Man* (Cambridge, Massachusetts, 1954).

HOEBEL, E. A. *The Political Organisation and Law-Ways of the Comanche Indians*, American Anthropological Association, Memoir 54 (Menasha, Wisconsin, 1940).

HOGBIN, H. *Law and Order in Polynesia* (London, 1934).

HOGBIN, H. 'Shame: Social Conformity in a New Guinea Village', *Oceania*, vol. 17 (1947), 4.

HOLMBERG, A. R. *Nomads of the Longbow* (New York, 1969).

KOCH, K. F. *War and Peace in Jalemo* (New Haven, 1974).

KROEBER, A. L. *Zuni Kin and Clan* (New York, 1917).

LEE, R. 'What Hunters Do for a Living', LEE and DEVORE (eds), *Man the Hunter*.

LEE, R. and DEVORE, I. (eds), *Man the Hunter* (Chicago, 1968).

LEWIS, I. *A Pastoral Democracy* (London, 1961).

LEWIS, I. *Social Anthropology in Perspective* (Harmondsworth, 1976).

LLEWELLYN, K. N. and HOEBEL, E. A. *The Cheyenne Way* (Norman, 1941).

MCINTYRE, A. 'Is understanding religion compatible with believing it?', HICK (ed.) *Faith and the Philosophers* (London, 1964).

MAINE, H. *Ancient Law* (London, 1861).

MAIR, L. P. *Primitive Government* (Harmondsworth, 1962).

MALINOWSKI, B. *Coral Gardens and Their Magic* (London, 1935).

MALINOWSKI, B. *Crime and Custom in Savage Society* (London, 1926).

MALINOWSKI, B. Introduction to HOGBIN, *Law and Order in Polynesia*.

MARSHALL, L. 'Sharing, Talking and Giving: Relief of Social Tension among !Kung Bushmen', *Africa*, vol. 31 (1961), 231–49.

MAUSS, M. *Essai sur le don* (Paris, (1925); English trans. by CUNNISON, I. *The Gift* (London, 1954).

MIDDLETON, J. *The Kikuyu and Kamba of Kenya* (London, 1953).

MORGAN, L. H. *Ancient Society* (New York, 1877).

MURPHY, R. F. 'Intergroup Hostility and Social Cohesion', *American Anthropologist*, vol. 59 (1957), 1018–35.

NADEL, S. F. 'Social Control and Self-Regulation', *Social Forces*, (1953), 265.

NADER, L. (ed.) *Law in Culture and Society* (Chicago, 1969).

OTTERBEIN, K. 'Internal War: A Cross-cultural Study', *American Anthropologist*, vol. 70 (1968), 277–89.

POSPISIL, L. *Anthropology of Law* (New York, 1971).

POSPISIL, L. *Kapauku Papuans and Their Law* (New Haven, 1958).

RADCLIFFE-BROWN, A. R. 'Primitive Law', *Encyclopaedia of the Social Sciences*, vol. 9 (New York, 1933), 202–6.

RADCLIFFE-BROWN, A. R. 'Social Sanctions', *Encyclopaedia of the Social Sciences*, vol. 13 (New York, 1933), 531–4.

RAPPAPORT, R. *Pigs for the Ancestors: Ritual in the Ecology of a New Guinea People* (New Haven, 1967).

RASMUSSEN, K. *Across Arctic America* (New York, 1927).

REAY, M. 'Changing Conventions of Dispute Settlement in the Minj Area', EPSTEIN (ed.), *Contention and Dispute*.

REDFIELD, R. 'Primitive Law', BOHANNAN (ed.), *Law and Warfare*.

RIVERS, W. H. R. *Social Organisation* (London, 1924).

ROBERTS, S. with COMAROFF, J. L. 'Chiefly Decision and the Devolution of Property in a Tswana Chiefdom', COHEN and SHACK (eds), *Politics in Leadership* (Oxford, 1978).

ROSCOE, J. 'Notes on the Bageshu' *Journal of the Royal Anthropological Institute*, vol. 39 (1909), 181–95.

SALMOND, J. *Jurisprudence* (London, 1902).

SCHAPERA, I. *A Handbook of Tswana Law and Custom* (London, 1938).

SCHAPERA, I. *Married Life in an African Tribe* (London, 1940).

SCHAPERA, I. *Tribal Legislation among the Tswana of the Bechuanaland Protectorate* (London, 1943).

SIMMEL, G. *Conflict*, trans. WOLFF (Illinois, 1955).

STANNER, W. 'Continuity and Schism in an African Tribe – A Review', *Oceania*, vol. 29 (1959), 208–17.

SUMNER, W. G. *Folkways* (Boston, Massachusetts, 1906).

Sunday Times, The. *The Thalidomide Children and the Law: A Report* (London, 1973).

TURNBULL, C. *Wayward Servants* (London, 1966).

TURNER, V, *Schism and Continuity in an African Society* (Manchester, 1957).

TWINING, W. L. *The Place of Customary Law in the National Legal Systems of East Africa* (Chicago, 1964).

VAN VELZEN, T. with VAN WETERING, W. 'Residence, Power Groups and Intra-Societal Aggression: An Enquiry into the

Conditions Leading to Peacefulness in Non-Stratified Societies', *Int. Arch. Ethnog.*, vol. 49 (1960), 169–200.

WARNER, E. *Trial by Sasswood* (London, 1955).

WEBER, M. *The Methodology of the Social Sciences*, trans. SHILS and FINCH (New York, 1949).

WEYER, E. M. *The Eskimos* (New Haven, 1932).

WILLIAMS, F. E. *Orokaiva Society* (London, 1930).

WINCH, P. 'Understanding a Primitive Society', *American Philosophical Quarterly*, vol. 1 (1964), pp. 307–24.

WOODBURN, J. C. 'Ecology, nomadic movement and the composition of the local group among hunters and gatherers: an East African example and its implications', UCKO, TRINGHAM and DIMBLEBY (eds), *Man, Settlement and Urbanism* (London, 1972), pp. 193–206.

YOUNG, M. *Fighting with Food* (Cambridge, 1971).

Index